WILD
BLUE
YONDER

✪

In memory of SATOR SANCHEZ

Leslie J. Tyler

Author in 1944.

WILD
BLUE
YONDER

★

An Adventure of Hitler's Hostages

LESLIE J. TYLER

Crystal Publishing
Grawn, Michigan

Additional copies of this book may be ordered
through bookstores or by sending $12.95
plus $2.75 for postage and handling to:
Publishers Distribution Service
121 East Front Street, Suite 203
Traverse City, MI 49684
1-800-345-0096

Publisher's Cataloging-in-Publication Data

Tyler, Leslie J., 1919–
    Wild blue yonder : an adventure of Hitler's hostages /
    Leslie J. Tyler.–Grawn, MI : Crystal Pub.,
        p.   cm.
    Includes bibliograhphical references.
    ISBN 0-9631159-0-1
    1. Tyler, Leslie J., 1919– 2. World War, 1939-1945–Personal
    narratives, American. 3. World War, 1939-1945–Aerial
    operations, American. 4. World War, 1939-1945–Prisoners and
    prisons, German. 5. United States. Air Force–Biography. I. Title.

D811.T95   1992
940./544/973 [B] [92] dc20   91-76311

Manufactured in the United States of America
Book Design: Alex Moore/PDS

For my daughter, Leslie Jo Tyler,
whose early encouragement
motivated me to complete this book.

ACKNOWLEDGMENTS

✪

David W. Parrish, Jr., retired Vice Chairman of the Michie Company, for his helpful commentary. And without the help of my sister, Alice Nowell, I would still be typing the first chapter.

The major events described in this book are factual. However, some of the minor events, e.g. who did what and when, have been altered to provide continuity to the narrative and give it coherence. The intent was not to diminish nor enhance the role of any of the individuals mentioned.

The photographs were provided by Erwin H. Eckert, Historian of the 301st Veterans Association, P.O. Box 160455, San Antonio, TX, 78280.

PREFACE

✪

Dr. Eugene Sullivan, the first president of Dow Corning, was inspirational. Even at age ninety he continued to exhort his scientists "never look back."

But old soldiers should look back. The author, as an old soldier, tries to focus the remembrances of close friends who died in world War II. These quiet heroes of tumultuous years departed so silently that they have virtually been forgotten. This book is a tribute to them.

CONTENTS

✪

Oh, I have slipped the surly bonds of earth....

....

.... put out my hand and touched the face of God!.

John Gillespie Magee, Jr.

WILD
BLUE
YONDER

★

✪

DUTT
DOWN AT SEA

Sometimes we called him "Dutt." He was Finlay K. Dutton — Iowa born and bred — Red Oak, Iowa. There he was in November, 1944, newly assigned to and sole occupant of tent ten. The tent was one of many located in an old olive grove near the village of Lucera, Italy and home for fliers of the 353rd Bomb Squadron. Dutton welcomed Art and Walt and me as we moved in on him. He rattled away in his peculiar style, making welcome with a heart as big as his ideas. Like I, he was a navigator and my tent mate for the next four months. That in itself would suffice to bring us close together. But, there was a deeper bond. The temper of his personality made me like him a little better each day. He was the only completely unselfish soldier I ever met.

The four of us became good friends as we pitched in to make the tent more liveable. I was the scrounger and a good one. My prize was a sixteen-foot section of sewer pipe that we "borrowed" for use as a stovepipe — along with a half drum for the stove and a jettisoned gasoline tank from a fighter plane for fuel storage. Now we would be warm for the winter weather that was beginning to shroud that section of Italy. We could heat water in our helmets for shaving and many were the piping-hot midnight snacks with the accompanying fresh hot coffee. Tent ten's stovepipe was the tallest structure in our tent city. It was a serious challenge to the P-38 fighter pilots in an adjacent squadron. A "buzz" of the 353rd was only a success if tent ten rocked.

Art (Snyder) was the titular leader of the four, because he was an airplane commander (and the oldest). Art's failings were cigarettes, whiskey and wild, wild women. He had a pair of boots that he handled with loving care. The boots were like the ones that William Holden wore in the movie "Picnic." When Art got drunk (often) the boots got muddy. How he worked those over until they shone once more. Despite the volumes of "gin and juice" that Art consumed at the nearby tar-papered officers' club, he was a great pilot once he hit the cockpit — maybe the best pilot in the squadron.

Walt (Eugene Walters) was Art's copilot and I was their navigator. Walt was a good-looking guy and a football hero from the University of Washington. His claim to fame was that his college girlfriend had just played her first small role in the Hollywood movie business and changed her name to Janis Paige. She was a beauty and we all admired the six pictures of her that Walt displayed. Walt's other claim to fame: he was the only person we ever met who could light his own farts and keep them burning.

In January a fifth airman moved into tent ten. He was Steven Butler and the third navigator in our small group. We called him "Butler, S." because there was another Butler in the squadron, who was labeled Butler, T. Butler, S. was tall, lean, sharp-beaked and fairly attractive. He was the only married man of the five — and he made marriage sound like a loving relationship. He talked, talked, talked — and fortunately had the sense of humor to make it tolerable. He had worked for Frigidaire and convinced himself and all of us never to take another assembly line job. One day I came into tent ten to find that Butler, S. had swapped his cot position for mine. I didn't say a word, but returned the cots to the former positions. We got along well after that.

Dutton had a talent for sketching. He said his parents encouraged him to "make marks" before he could write. His sketches were not art, but he had the artist's soul. One of his goals was to capture in a sketch a design that could be adopted as the official logo of the 353rd Bomb Squadron. He worked on that sketch off and on but was never fully satisfied. I liked to watch over his shoulder and never tired of seeing him bring a view to life with pencil and paper.

Dutt started the new year in style. On Christmas he had completed a dozen combat missions and was eligible for a week's rest leave. Somehow Walt (with no combat missions) got to accompany him. They went to Rome and Dutt, who was a Catholic, had a glimpse of the pope in St. Peter's Square on New Year's Day. Then Dutt and Walt went to the Isle of Capri for a few days. They hiked the hills and cliffs, visited the old monastery on top of one of the two hills that make up Capri. In the monastery, they talked to the young monk who was recording weather observations that dated back several centuries; they thrilled at the wild bus rides up the cliff side roadways. They visited the old villa that had been constructed for Tiberius Caesar; they took boat rides and viewed the ghostly beauty of the Blue Grotto and hummed the popular song "...'twas on the Isle of Capri..." They reveled in the luxury of the large bedrooms, the huge bathtubs and the grand bath towels. The countess invited them and dozens of other fliers to a balcony luncheon and made them feel that lovely women had not disappeared forever. But the reality of war brought them back to the cold, wet and muddy olive grove and the warmth of tent ten.

At first I was the ranking officer of the five second lieutenants in our tent. But in late January both Art and Dutt were promoted to first lieutenant. Dutt was a fine navigator and now his crew was selected to fly Squadron Lead. Dutt took it in stride. He and his crew flew six missions as the Squadron Lead crew.

One of these missions was most unusual. Normally departure on the bombing missions was in the morning. The Battle Order (BO) would be posted at 6 p.m. the night before. One morning at about 10 an orderly burst into tent ten and addressed Dutton with the message that he was to report to the briefing hut ready to fly in ten minutes. About thirty minutes later Dutt came back to the tent to get his sextant and oxygen mask. He was under orders to be completely mum, which he was. But you could detect the inner excitement that an interesting assignment brings. Dutt's plane took off at 2 p.m. as lead for only three B-17s. They disappeared, giving no clue to their destination as they headed out over the Adriatic. None of the planes had returned by the time darkness fell. Late the next afternoon Dutt appeared at the tent with an interesting tale.

It turned out that a mini civil war was raging in Greece as the Nazis withdrew their troops under pressure from the British. The civil war was to determine whether the Partisans or the Communists would seize power in Athens. Winston Churchill was determined to pre-empt the communists from establishing this foothold in Greece. He understood the real menace that the USSR would be after the war was over. At Churchill's request the 15th was flying ammunition into Athens for the beleaguered Partisans.

The three planes from Lucera were loaded with this ammunition. They flew a low-level mission down the length of the Adriatic and came in low to land at the Athens airport, which was held by the Partisans. Fortunately they avoided the several bomb craters on the runways. After landing they faced intermittent fire all night long. But the delivery was crucial and this mission was helpful in keeping one country from falling under the domination of a puppet Communist government. After sunup all thirty fliers helped clear debris from the upwind runway so they could get the hell out of there. They were truly unsung and unknown heroes who helped decide the fate of a nation.

After his promotion and successful leadership on the Athens mission, Finlay's crew was promoted to Group Leadership. They joined two other crews of the 353rd who held that responsibility. Captain Wine (Wino) the squadron's number one navigator checked Dutton on the procedure for the group rendezvous. It was a simple procedure, but an easy one to screw up. It was necessary to keep giving the pilot headings that would take the plane in a giant circle and complete the circle in exactly the correct time allotted. Not as easy as it sounds.

On March 4, they "suited up" and flew their first mission as a group lead. Officially they were the Deputy Group Lead plane on this mission to Zagreb. There were always two group lead planes – one flying point and the other in formation just to the right and behind the point plane. Both crews were briefed and both planes were equipped with the then-new radar navigational devices. Dutt's plane flew lead that day in another squadron. I flew that mission also — my second mission as Squadron Lead Navigator for the 353rd.

For the 301st B-17s the mission to Zagreb in Yugoslavia — exactly due north of our base in Italy was an extremely short run (but not a "milk run"). The heaviest German defenses were south of the target. The tactical plan was to fly the group past Zagreb and feint toward Graz in Austria, then swing rapidly south directly to the target — but coming in from the north and with a tailwind on the bomb run. The Zagreb defenses would relax as the group passed by and would have minimum opportunity to raise an effective flak barrage.

After the Group passed Zagreb and approached Graz my plane developed engine trouble and it became apparent the 353rd could not keep pace with the Group. The group dared not slow just for us because maximum speed on the bomb run was mandatory. Dutt led the group south toward Zagreb. I led the 353rd to our secondary target near Graz. We dropped our bombs and limped home

The Group came under very heavy fire over the Zagreb target and Dutt's lead plane was hit, losing the number one engine. They were forced to abandon the formation and headed alone directly south toward Italy and home base. As the plane crossed the Adriatic coast of Yugoslavia a second engine failed. The Aircraft Commander decided to "ditch" while they had two good engines left. This was SOP because the Royal Navy controlled the Adriatic even though the Germans held Yugoslavia.

Dutt died that day. In dying he was at his selfless best. A B-17 doesn't float very long and Dutt helped the enlisted crew members out of the plane first. The sea claimed another victim and I lost my best friend. My son's name is Bruce Dutton Tyler. Sometimes we call him Dutt.

✪

CHAPTER 2

THE TENTH MAN
A B-17 CREW MEMBER

Ten fine young men met each other for the first time in the summer of 1944. They met in Sioux City. They were to become a team—the ten-member crew of a B-17. This Boeing Flying Fortress was the fabled plane reverently called the "big-assed bird" by those who flew it so proudly. It was the single most important factor in the defeat of Hitler and his "...*morgen die Welt*" Nazis.

From California and Pennsylvania they came. From Nebraska and Texas and Binghamton, New York and Cleveland, Ohio. They trained at Hondo, Texas and Las Vegas—at Kelly Field and Bakersfield—at Alamogordo and Denver. They were products of a most effective educational program. They became pilots and navigators—bombardiers and radio operators—and especially they became gunners—chin gunners, tail gunners, ball gunners, top turret gunners, and waist gunners.

There was Emil Yovich. He was the tail gunner. He always joked that he was the only one who knew where they had been. Emil became a solid member of the crew. He was called Hap. He was young, but looked old. That can happen to tail gunners. Hap hailed from Fairview Village, Ohio on the east side of Cleveland. Lake was one of the waist gunners. He was unflappable—the ideal gunner. For him life was an adventure every day. Dick lived in the little village of York, Nebraska so Sioux City corn country was familiar territory to him. The other waist gunner was Taylor, a quiet and effective crew member. Taylor was one of the two married men on the crew. He and his bride spent his furlough at their home in Lufkin, Texas.

Dale Thornton was the pilot. He was the second married man on the crew. Thornton was as self assured as any pilot who ever flew a B-17. What a comfort that was to the crew! Dale talked often about his wife, Lucille, and she was prolific in sending him letters. She lived in Los Angeles. The copilot was Ed Narracci. From the very first day the crew started calling him "The Face"—talk about tall, dark, and handsome. Before pilot training he had been a radio operator and was a very brainy guy—the perfect partner for Thornton. Ed (or Ted) was from the mile-high city of Denver. The bombardier was Rury, from New York State. He was thin, tall, blonde, aloof and an excellent bombardier.

The navigator was Lt. Bass, a very soft-spoken Texan, as was the second Texan, Taylor. Bass was a helluva good navigator—but never believed that he was. The chief engineer was Sgt. Schratz—competent, cool, quiet, and dependable. On the ground the engineer was responsible for unequivocal communication with the ground crews who serviced the plane. In the air the engineer manned the top turret guns. So, in more than one way, the engineer was the pivotal crew member. The ball gunner was John Scott. He was not a hail-fellow-well-met, but he was tall, gutsy, tough, wiry and he liked being a ball gunner. This was an arduous assignment during the hours-long missions that the 17 flew. Maybe being in the womb position all that time compensated for the claustrophobic environment.

The tenth man was Sgt. Gene "Squeaky" Buckel. He was the radio operator and the last man assigned to the crew. He could speak Morse code better than most could speak English.

Even before they met there was a bond between the ten. Each link was forged as one by one in airfields around the U.S. they read their new orders which assigned them to B-17 phase training. Almost every flier in the USAAF regarded the Fort as a "glory" plane. In the first days of the war Colin Kelly was the heroic pilot of the first B-17 lost in combat. But in subsequent battles many B-17's survived almost intolerable punishment. The mystique surrounding the plane began to emerge. By 1944 the B-17 was the plane that combat crews yearned to fly—although its younger, larger brother, the Boeing B-29, was becoming a contender.

In flight the Fortress, with its magnificent upswept tail, was a thing of beauty to behold. With a wing span of 100 feet and a length of 75 feet it had an artistic symmetry. Its gross weight was 30,000 pounds, truly in the "heavy" bomber class. Its range was nearly 4,000 miles and its service ceiling was 35,000 feet. Powered by four Wright cyclone engines, one of which could keep the plane aloft, the plane was the ideal candidate for the offensive by air against Germany. The last model, the G, had a chin turret which increased the number of fifty caliber guns to thirteen—truly a "flying fortress." Nearly 13,000 of these marvelous bombers were built, most by Boeing where the plane was designed, but almost 3,000 each by Douglas and Lockheed. The 13,000 planes were built at a cost about equivalent to the cost of only two B-2 "stealth" bombers.

Day after good day the crew would fly their B-17. Most of the "missions" were designed to teach the pilots to fly a tight formation. A tight formation of a squadron of B-17's was a fearsome target for a Luftwaffe fighter pilot. They preferred to go after the B-24's or the B-17 stragglers. The first experience in formation flying was very scary. In all previous flying the objective was to keep a very safe distance from all other aircraft. Now the objective was to bring the plane close to the adjacent plane (50-50; fifty feet wing tip to wing tip and nose to tail). This one other plane from which the pilots took their formation position was the guidon (or wingman). Getting into the formation is the most frightening. The plane approaches the guidon from the rear and below. At first it moves in too close. By reducing and increasing throttle the pilots bring the plane into position by gradually decreasing the amplitude of the fore and aft motion of the plane relative to the guidon. After dozens of hours of formation flying the apprehension disappears. In fact, it becomes a comfort to look across to the adjacent plane and see the faces of the other crew.

Some of the practice missions were to the Badlands near Rapid City—an exquisitely emptied area of the U.S.,—ideal for live gunnery practice. There were also simulated gunnery missions with camera guns when the "attacking fighters" were flown by pilots in training at Hastings, Nebraska. Even in practice a fighter plane coming in at a bomber can be a harrowing sight to the bomber crew. The relative motion of the two planes as they converged and diverged made the fighters look as if they were gliding sideways—and it all happens in an instant. But, it gave the gunners the kind of practice they needed most. The most difficult aspect was to teach the gunners "to lead the fighter always toward the rear of their own bomber."

Some of the missions were practice runs for the bombardier. The plane was equipped with the famed Norden Bombsight. Rury was very familiar with this device. When it is activated the bombardier is flying the plane and not the pilots. To hit a target from six miles high it is essential that the plane be flying straight and level. If that is the situation, the Norden compensates for altitude, speed, temperature, drift and distance from the target. But the bombardier had to fly the plane, sight the aiming point and release the bombs at the exact instant required. Rury's scores were always among the best in the group of thirty crews who were in this phase of training.

Some of the missions were designed to test and whet the skill of the Navigator. Lt. Bass always came through. He liked pilotage type navigation the best because it was the only form of navigation in those years wherein the navigator knows where the plane is located. Most of the missions tested him in dead reckoning. This was like playing a stimulating and challenging game. Bass would be heady after three hours of dead reckoning to look down and see the Sioux City landing field exactly at his ETA. He struggled with the one celestial navigation mission. In sighting stars with a sextant at right angles to the line of flight, even a two degree roll of the bomber on its longitudinal axis can throw the line of position off by more than a hundred miles. But Bass took the crew on a 500-mile flight and did well enough so that the mission did not have to be repeated. This was propitious because it was one of the last requirements before the crew would be okayed for a combat assignment. All of this final-phase training took only three months. The crew was combat-ready and eager.

First they moved to Lincoln, Nebraska. That was the depot for making final assignments to theaters of combat. The crew looked longingly at the line of brand-new shiny B-17's that crews would fly from Lincoln to the destination, often Europe. Sometimes the pathway was via Brazil, Ascension Island, Africa and then to Italy and the 15th Air Force. Sometimes the pathway would be via Newfoundland, Iceland, Ireland to England and the 8th Air Force.

But there were twice as many crews as there were brand new Flying Forts. So Thornton and his nine teammates were bitterly disappointed to learn that they would travel from Lincoln by train rather than in their very own bomber.

First there were ten glorious days of furlough and goodbyes. Off they went to 10 different families, to ten different towns, to nine different states.

After the furlough the crew was "processed," receiving brand new flying gear, sextants and boots, light flying suits, heavy flying suits, A-2 jackets, B-4 bags, even gas masks. It was all deluxe for combat's finest. There was a last night on the town. They will never forget the Cornhusker Hotel and the Stites beer.

From Lincoln there was a 60-hour train trip on a dirty troop train. They headed east—so it looked like Europe or the CBI. The port of embarkation was Camp Patrick Henry, Virginia. What a motivational name! Camp PH was delightful—a shady pine-tree-studded camping ground and the weather was Indian summer. The crew relaxed, rested, waited, and looked ahead. It wasn't long. On 21 October the crew boarded one of those six knot Liberty Ships, the USS John Blair. (Who was John Blair? He was a signer of the U.S. Constitution.) The John Blair sailed that day from Hampton Roads. The crew at first was a bit somber as the U.S. of A. disappeared from their view. All had been well treated on boarding by the USO ladies, who provided cookies and candy, Bibles and paper back books by the hundreds, stationery and pens, decks of cards, checkers and chess sets. The bridge players got at it right away and kept it up day after day after day.

Even the captain of the John Blair did not know the ship's destination. So Lt. Bass used his sextant to plot the course on the high seas. The John Blair was one of a convoy—maybe 150 ships— a huge convoy. First they headed toward Bermuda, trying to skirt an October hurricane. Talk about seasick airmen (almost

100 percent). Hampton Roads is near the 37th parallel. Bass tracked the Blair going due east for several days but zigging and zagging a little. This was head-on toward the Straits of Gibralter. That started a few rumors about destinations. Later the convoy drifted south toward the bulge of Africa. That started a new rumor about destination. But after 19 days just off the African coast a destroyer came alongside and passed over destination orders for the John Blair—Oran, Africa.

The 19 days were a wonderment for the crew, none of whom had ever been on the ocean before. They endlessly enjoyed the lure of the sea. Monotonous, yes—but there were beautiful sights: glistening flying fish, easy-sailing gulls, torpedo-like porpoises, the phosphorescent glow of the bow waves at night, the deep blue of the Gulf Stream, the flat horizon dotted by a hundred ships in convoy, the picturesque miniature storms and rain showers, and the rainbows they often cast, the glow of a fiery sun dipping down under the rim of the sea, or the glow of a full moon shimmering on the water as it ascends, or even the bitter black of a moonless night when blackout regulations were enforced, the twinkling stars of phosphorescence that boil up in the turbulent water on dark nights and the closeness of the stars at sea with nothing hindering the view. It was all okay.

On the sixteenth day out FDR was reelected—for an unprecedented fourth term. The few of the crew over 21 had already voted for him by absentee ballot back in early October. Soon the convoy steamed through the Straits and past the "Rock," a neat sight. The John Blair then left the convoy since the Mediterranean had been cleared of U-boats. It arrived at Oran after 20 days at sea. The crew disembarked and spent the night ashore in a miserable tent city. But there were two bonuses. One was a <u>fresh</u> shower after 20 days of salt water showers. The second was a movie—"Two Girls and a Sailor." In how many movies did Van Johnson appear in a World War II uniform? Did he ever serve?

The next morning the crew boarded a dirty, old, decrepit French ship, the Sidi Brahim-Marseilles. It was discovered, just in time, that there was no food aboard. So, back to Oran. This time the crew was able to see the city. For all of the crew this was their first foreign city. From the harbor it is a beautiful port—a horseshoe curve of distinguished buildings and a shrine of some sort pushing out of the one hillside above the city. Rugged terrain surrounds the town.

In the city the crew tried to bargain (in French) for sandwiches, drank the ubiquitous cokes, found that all the stores were closed, observed that even tiny Arab children were trying to buy American money (for the Germans) and pimping and pandering indiscriminately—or being skillful and unabashed at the art of pickpocketing. The architecture up close looked even more foreign. The streets were narrow and dirty and full of soldiers and sailors with multi-countried uniforms. Nobody located a "den of iniquity"—but for the fact that they were allowed in town only one day. They all said they would go back someday. None ever did.

Two days later they returned to the Sidi. The food that had been loaded belied the French reputation for culinary excellence. The next day the Sidi docked at Algiers, la premiere Ville du Nord Afrique. But nobody could leave the ship—for three long, miserable days. On November 16 the Sidi headed east from Algiers, hugging the African coast. The weather was clear, warm and sunny. Spirits picked up. On the 17th the ship passed Cape Bon and sailed close to the island of Pantelleria. This island had recently made Air Force history. It was the first battle in which the enemy had surrendered to an attack only by Air Force flying personnel. Who needs the infantry? Next was Malta, which slipped by the port side at night. Malta had made RAF history. Three incredibly old, tired, but not obsolete seaplanes, the only air defense of Malta, had defended the island for sixty days against the entire Italian Air Force, which before the war was as vaunted as the Luftwaffe. These three planes were named Faith, Hope and Charity, and their pilots really deserved the Churchillian accolade that was bestowed on the defenders of England in the summer of 1940.

The next day the crew witnessed what seemed like a mirage. It was Mt. Aetna, so far distant that it seemed to be hovering above the horizon and disconnected from the earth below. That evening Aetna erupted—a glorious 4th of July sight for soldiers who had never before seen a volcano. On the 19th the Sidi docked at Augusta, Sicily to take on fuel. The skeletons of destroyed planes and ships filled this harbor.

On November 20, the ship slipped through the Straits of Messina, where Sicily comes within kissing distance of Italy. By now the crew members were confident that the assignment would be to the Fifteenth Air Force, sometimes referred to as "the forgotten Air Force." North from the Straits went the Sidi and later that day steamed into Naples harbor. The crew disembarked as they took in the natural beauty of this wonderful harbor. Here and there a hulk of a partially sunken ship protruded to spoil the view. But most of the signs of war had been erased. The next stop was a Replacement Depot located in Caserta, a neighbor of Naples but inland. Caserta was the headquarters of the 15th as well as the residence of the Italian King, who had signed the surrender agreement for Italy the year before.

The crew spent four very interesting days at Caserta, interesting because their only duty was to wait—wait for an assignment from this "reppel deppel." The best assignment, Thornton concluded, would be at Headquarters, for the 15th had ousted King Victor from his summer palace and taken over this grandiose building. The first day was used for a visit to see the City of Naples. They had seen the beautiful harbor and that part of the city visible from the water. Naples is built like a huge horseshoe with the harbor at the center and the buildings sprawl back and upwards steeply from the waterfront. The city was not damaged too noticeably by the war. So in most ways it was beautiful. But there was a tarnish beneath the sheen. The four years since Italy had declared war on France after the Nazis defeated France had left scars on Italy and on this city also. But for a day it was a treat to be a Neapolitan.

The second day was an adventure for Bass and Narracci and another navigator, P. T. Taylor. They decided to try to get to Pompeii. They started by hitchhiking. The first ride was in an army truck and then in an army automobile. Then they hailed a General Patton tank which was coming down the corridor. After a ride in this behemoth all concluded that the B-17 was their baby. A tank on a cobblestone road is noisier than two B-17's. After the tank ride they were given a short jog in a horse drawn carriage. Then they got another jeep to take them to the railroad station. The train pulled out of Naples before noon. To say that it was crowded was a gross understatement. After all of the paying customers were jammed into the cars and seats, a second group of passengers boarded. These were mostly young Italians. They clambered aboard and strove for the best spots on the exterior of the cars. The roof was the prime target, but dozens of brave souls were hanging from the steel rail ladders at the ends of the car. Bass wondered how many might not survive the short trip. But for the youthful riders it was taken in the spirit of adventure.

When the train reached Pompeii the smoldering mountain dominated the horizon. The plume from Vesuvius seemed ominous, although all day it was mostly quiescent. In Italian Narracci hailed an old man who said he could speak English and would be the guide. Off they went on foot. The old man proved to be very knowledgeable about the history of the old city, so renowned in book and cinema. He regaled his visitors with stories of the ancients, that seemed so plausible as he told them. The fabric of the stories lay in the discoveries made by the excavation of the old ruins, remarkably preserved by the layers of volcanic ash that crushed the life from the city and the citizens so long ago. Pompeii, like many ancient cities, reveled in the sinful life. The logo most surely was the "winged male genitalia" signs that pointed the way to the many houses where stayed the "ladies of the night." Both Bass and Narracci were particularly intrigued by the house of the Brothers Vetti. Here stayed the "gentlemen of the night" ...for the lady patrons.

The Italian guide asked if they liked opera because the damaged San Carlos Opera House in Naples had been refurbished enough to reopen that week. The opera was Rigoletto. He added that when Verdi was asked about his personal favorite opera he replied "Throw away all my other operas and call me Rigoletto." Narracci thanked the guide (in Italian) for this advice. Each chipped in to pay for his services and they wandered back to await the dinky little train. Back in Caserta there was much discussion about the Pompeii visit and reopening of the Opera

House. They decided to attend the performance of Rigoletto the next night, which they did along with several other members of the crew. It was a rousing performance and an introduction to high music for many of them. One bomb-damaged wall of the theater was not completely repaired so there was plenty of fresh air. For some of the crew this may have been the only opera they ever attended.

The last day at the 19th Replacement Depot was Thanksgiving. There was turkey with trimmings for all—the last really good meal for some time to come. On the day after Thanksgiving the crew moved by truck in a memorable, exciting, almost thrilling ride across the boot of Italy. Up hill and down dale it was a rough, cold ride weaving in and out of ox-drawn and motorized Italian vehicles with all the artistry a GI driver possesses. They noted again the effects of the war—blown-out bridges in repair—blown-up buildings and the endless filth and poverty of the Italian population. But all of the FO-465-JQ-11 shipment arrived to be assigned to the 353rd Squadron of the 301st Bomb Group of the Fifth Wing of the 15th Air Force.

The location was just east of Lucera, Italy and due west from Foggia—an air base in the "spur" of Italy's boot . It was an ideal spot for an air base—flat and easily identifiable because of the large Lake Lessina to the north as well as the hook-like peninsula of Termoli that jutted into the Adriatic. In the next weeks the pilots and navigator had several familiarization training missions. Bass imprinted in his mind the key landmarks surrounding the Lucera field that was the Squadron home. Both Thornton and Narracci could head directly for this field from any point on the Adriatic coast where they might make the landfall on returning from the missions.

And the crew were given information in familiarization briefings about the progress of the war and the strategies of the 15th Air Force. The primary strategy was to knock out all the German oil refineries, all of which were within striking distance of the 15th's B-17's. The secondary strategy was to destroy the railroad marshalling yards as support for the Russian offensive which was grinding westward toward Berlin.

The "oil knockout punch" had been adopted as primary strategy several months earlier. From June to August, the Fifteenth had mounted its most massive raids against an old target, Ploesti in Romania. These raids destroyed the "cracking" facilities, which converted crude oil into gasoline. This meant that the crude had to be transported to refineries located in Austria, Hungary and Czechoslovakia—all within range of the Fifteenth bombers. The strategy was magnificent. In the period June 1 to September 1, the availability of aviation fuel plummeted. Albert Speer reported on September 1 that he needed 50,000,000 gallons and only 10,000,000 were available. This may sound like a lot but was about two day's usage by the 15th Air Force, for example. In the same report he specified that aircraft production was at a new peak. The Luftwaffe was getting more airplanes, but no fuel.

Even in 1990, despite U.S. vulnerability to the OPEC bandits (remember 1973), our country has no capability for manufacturing synthetic oil. Fifty years ago German industry developed this capability and this made them much less dependent on crude oil. There were eight large synthetic oil refineries where the Germans converted the massive deposits of brown coal of Silesia into oil by reaction with hydrogen gas. Seven of the eight synthetic oil refineries were located at Brux (the largest), Blechhammer, Regensburg, Linz, Moosbierbaum, Wiener Neustadt, and Vienna, all within range of the 15th. The eighth was at Ruhland near Berlin, just outside of the known range of the 15th bombers, but within range of the 8th Air Force, located in England.

The oil strategy, already a big success, had a value to the 15th more evident each month. Despite the fact that the Germans were building more airplanes than ever, the Luftwaffe had not mounted a fighter interception of the 15th since mid-November, 1944. A good thing too, because the crews were now told that the Luftwaffe had introduced a radically new fighter—a plane without a propeller, a jet plane that could fly 600 mph, far faster than our Lightnings and Mustangs. The plane was the Me 262. Intelligence had no pictures or aircraft identification silhouettes as were available for the other Luftwaffe fighters. There was only an artist's sketch—and stories. One claimed that an Me 262 in a single fast pass had shot down 3 B-17's. The gunners referred to the jet planes as "blow jobs"—a little disdain often offsets a little disquiet.

By December 1 the crew was ready. But, in the next two weeks they were "scratched" three times from the Battle Order (a new meaning for BO). Their life on the ground was settling into a routine. They lived in tents and it was easy to tell that it was going to be a tough winter. There was no snow but it was cold and wet—and the mud was omnipresent. The meals at the mess hall were devoid of delight. The breakfasts were deadly. At his first breakfast Bass asked to be passed the scrambled eggs. There was complete silence—and all at the table turned to stare at Bass. He understood the stare when his fork bounced from the rubbery omelette. Thereafter he suspected that this same omelette was reheated and served day after day.

Each man was issued two blankets—not much protection for the coming winter nights. All of these new squadron members quickly engaged in the macabre practice of soliciting inclusions in the "wills" of the men who had been there awhile. The old timers possessed lots of "goodies" and top on the list were the down-filled sleeping bags and the soft leather RAF boots.

Because all missions flown took the planes over the Adriatic an almost daily ritual was "ditching practice." There was a mockup plane adjacent to the tent area for that purpose. In this practice Thornton would give the order "prepare to ditch." Then Bass would relay the ditching position latitude and longitude to the radio operator. Buckel would transmit this twice and then lock the transmitting key down and on. In the meantime the eight members other than the pilots went to the waist and sat down snuggled in line facing aft with the biggest, strongest man with his back to the bulkhead. After the "crash" the routine was to scramble out of the plane and inflate the two rubber dinghies aboard. Another practice, mostly a mental exercise, was to react instantly to a procedure for exiting the plane if the "bail-out bell" rang. Bass, in particular, went through this action in his mind's eye several times a day. It became an instinctive maneuver after a while.

The big day was December 17. The night before they were posted on the BO and it held. They were up at 4 a.m.—early chow, roll call, and briefing: briefing about flak, fighters, radio codes, about escort and emergency landing fields, about weather, about escape procedures and especially about the target and flight plan. From briefing it was a truck ride through the mud to pick up the personal gear. Each crew member had a locker storage at the flight line and a zippered barracks-type bag for all the gear needed aboard the plane. Then to the plane—Aircraft #429 this day. The squadron would put up ten planes on this mission. Thornton's crew would be in the "tail end Charlie" position, the last plane to take off, and the least desirable of the ten spots. It was reserved for rookies and goof-offs. The planes were parked on a hardstand near the single runway. With only one runway there was always a cross wind for takeoff and landing.

The target today was Blechhammer North—a synthetic oil refinery located near the "three corners" where the borders of Poland, Czechoslovakia and Germany met (pre-war borders). The target affirmed the dominant strategy of the 15th Air Force about which they had been briefed—"Deny the Wehrmacht and Luftwaffe their sources of fuel." At the War's end it was confirmed that pursuing this strategy did more to end the war than any other single military strategy.

Bass had his course plotted on his maps but knew that Thornton would be following his guidon today. The rendezvous point was the island of Vis, off the coast of Yugoslavia. They made this on schedule. From Vis the squadron, now a part of the group, headed northeast past Zagreb and across the Hungarian border. The planes continued to climb. The bombardier on the 17 is responsible for oxygen discipline. At 10,000 feet Rury gave the call to the crew to don oxygen masks. Thereafter he would ask for an "oxygen check" every five minutes.

There is a drop in temperature of four degrees for every thousand feet of altitude and it starts to get cold at 10,000 feet. This was the first time that the crew had ever been in such a large formation. The endless sight of B-17's up ahead was a wonderment and a pride. There was considerable cloudiness as the planes started to cross Yugoslavia, with the clouds well below the formation. To the southeast Bass alerted the crew they could get a partial view of the Andaric Alps which are the feature of the rugged terrain—the peaks they could see through the broken clouds were snow-covered but were nowhere near as high as the more well-known mounts of Switzerland.

The course they followed was selected to avoid flak emplacements except at the targets, where it was a certainty the planes would come under fire. During the briefing Bass had been issued a new map with an updated designation of all areas on the map protected by anti-aircraft guns. But on this mission the course took the Squadron over the Hungarian city of Nagykanitsa, which according to Intelligence was flak-free. All of a sudden there were puffs of black flak bursts up ahead and to the sides. The plane got only a few small holes in one wing, an easy encounter for the first time under fire. It had happened so fast and was over so quickly the crew hardly had a chance to be tense. Bass made a mental note to be wary of Nagykanitsa evermore—and that flak guns other than those known to Intelligence could be down there anywhere.

Shortly after the flak incident the cloud cover diminished somewhat and Bass got his first look at a landmark he would see often. It was Lake Balaton, a lake so large that it was unmistakable—a great aid to the navigators. The view of Balaton gave Bass a firm "fix" so that he could correct his dead reckoning position a little. They were about four minutes behind schedule. The planes continued to climb as they crossed Hungary and headed into Czechoslovakia. Down went the temperature but the garb kept them warm. They wore light underwear, then long johns, covered by a light flying suit. Aboard the plane one donned a thin electrically-heated flying suit including heated slippers and gloves. Over this was a heavy flying suit and this was covered by a very snug parachute harness. The harness was tailor-made for each crew member to fit as tightly as possible. Over this was a "Mae West," an inflatable life preserver, in case ditching in the Adriatic was necessary. By the time they reached full altitude the temperature would be minus 50 degrees F at 30,000 feet. It was a ten-minute struggle to extract a cold penis through all these layers of gear. You learned never to drink any liquids for twelve hours before a mission. That way it was possible to go the ten mission hours without having to urinate. The alternative, enuresis, was more than embarrassing. It could "short" the electrically heated suit, with near shocking consequences.

The group passed Bratislava at the southern sector of Czechoslovakia and headed north across this country toward the Initial Point (IP) of the bomb run. The IP was Wurbenthal, about 40 miles or eight minutes WSW from the target.

To describe some of the experiences on this mission it is necessary to describe the role of RADAR. Radar as a life-and-death technology came of age in the summer of 1940. The British Radar innovators had installed radar stations along the eastern coast of Britain. The Germans were somewhat familiar with the technology but failed to realize its importance. That summer radar and the consummate skill of the RAF pilots decided the outcome of the Battle of Britain. You can bet the Germans were impressed and by 1944 they installed numerous radar tracking stations. These stations could determine the number, direction, height and speed of approaching bombers. The Germans protected all of their important targets with flak guns which could be aimed with radar. This technique of antiaircraft fire is only effective when the bombers are flying "straight and level at constant speed"—like on a bomb run.

Yankee ingenuity had unearthed a very simple counteroffensive for the German radar tracking stations. Each plane carried a large supply of "chaff" or "winnow." This was a multitude of clumps of tiny strips of metal foil—almost identical to the Christmas tree trimming all of the crew members had used so often in the days of "peace." Then, minutes before the plane was to arrive at the IP, Bass would give the signal to the waist gunners to "throw out the chaff." Lake would anchor himself to the bulkhead with a rope, open the door and start heaving. As the chaff hit the windstream it would spread out as individual strips forming a thin silvery cloud. To the German Radar operators these clouds of chaff looked like the blip made by a bomber. Thus, on cloudy days it was an effective disruption of radar interception.

They arrived at the IP about ten minutes late. By now the cloud cover was 100 percent. The dense cloud cover had its advantages and disadvantages. The advantage, of course, was that the antiaircraft guns, aimed by radar, would be more random and less accurate. Similarly, the bombing, aimed by radar would be less accurate. Only the lead planes were equipped with this radar bombing capability, usually called "MICKEY." The equipment and the bombardiers and navigators were improving monthly. The 15th AF was a pioneer of this "blind bombing."

The course to the target gave them a strong tail wind so that the time over the heavy defenses would be minimal. It was a long eight minutes for the inexperienced crew. As "tail end Charlie" their plane was the last one for the gunners down there to aim at. As the briefing indicated, the flak was very heavy. And it seemed heavier to the last plane because all the previous flak bursts had not yet dissipated and the new ones were arriving constantly. Each crew member adopted a mental set for the bomb run in a different way. The Roman Catholic discipline helped some. Many a "Hail Mary" was uttered during this most dangerous time of the mission. And, as in foxholes, there are no atheists on bomb runs. Helping add a little sense of security were the flak suits, which were worn only on the bomb run because they were so heavy—many tiny metal plates sewn into an apron-like garment for both front and back. For one thing, struggling to move around in a flak suit took your mind off the flak. Only for the last four minutes were they surrounded by these black puffs. You could not hear them. But you could feel the shock wave of the close ones.

Rury had his twelve 500-pound bombs set on the intervalometer to drop one every two seconds. He did not have to use the bomb sight because the procedure that day called for the bombardiers of the six follow planes to start "bombs away" when the lead plane dropped its first bomb. By this synchronization there were seven RDX bombs heading for the target every two seconds (RDX was a new explosive developed at Penn State that was more powerful than TNT). After the twelfth bomb fell Rury gave the "bombs away" response and Thornton rallied right with the Squadron and headed southeast out of Flak Alley.

Bombs Away.

B-17 in Flak.

It was only after "bombs away" that the crew became aware that there were dogfights in the distance. The Luftwaffe interceptors were FW 190's and ME 109's. But they were <u>outnumbered</u> by the P-38 Lightnings and the P-51 Mustangs—the fighter escort for the bombers. This was the first time in a month that the Luftwaffe had attempted to intercept the bombers. The bombers' "Little Friends," the fighter escort, did a superb job of intercepting the interceptors.

With this southerly course at that hour the plane was heading for the sun. The warming rays were welcome, especially to Rury and Bass in the nose, where the huge Plexiglas housing allowed full transmission. But Thornton and Narracci were warmed too, as was Schratz in the top turret. Only Yovich was colder on the way back.

With the flak behind them and fighters never getting close, the crew started to relax and savor the completion of the first bomb run. The clouds prevented anybody from seeing what might have happened to the target. And, of course, the one plane of each squadron designated as the photography plane could take no target pictures either. It would be a few days before a reconnaissance plane would record their hits and misses. The weather on the way home was the same—solid cloud cover at first but diminishing slowly as they moved south. Lake, who had never left Nebraska until a year ago, was flabbergasted to hear Bass tell the crew that they were now European travelers—having been in six countries that very day—Italy, Yugoslavia, Hungary, Czechoslovakia, Germany and Poland—and just missing Austria. Over Hungary the cloud cover was light and Bass got a second good look at Lake Balaton, fixing it forever in his mind. And, you can bet your cigar that the lead navigator missed Nagykanitsa by a comfortable margin.

All seven planes of Squadron 353 returned in formation and landed left plane first and right plane last. Thornton was the last to land and needed help from Narracci for the tricky cross wind landing. With the upwind wing tilted downwards a little and with the plane "crabbing" into the wind almost 20 degrees, they approached the landing strip. The latter was made of a series of heavy open grid iron plates that interlock mechanically and can be "solid" even when laid down over muddy terrain. Just before touchdown on this iron mat both pilots kick rudder hard and with full ailerons try to bring the plane into line with the runway. This tilts the upwind wing upwards and the plane lands on one wheel. Balanced there it would take but a gust of wind to flip the downwind wing into the ground. But this day the plane rolls along until gravity settles the upwind wheel to the metal strip.... Whew!

After landing the pilots headed for the pilot debriefing. Rury was excused from the bombardier debriefing because of the cloud cover over target. Bass was directed to the navigators' debriefing room for his comments on the lead navigator's performance. The enlisted men went directly to the Red Cross unit. Each crew member was first offered an ounce of whiskey—neat. Most were glad to swallow this old and traditional tranquilizer. But, they appreciated more the welcoming smiles of the Red Cross ladies and the hot coffee and hot doughnuts—and the banter with the men from the other crews who had been over Blechhammer that morning.

After debriefing it was almost supper time and they were hungry. Each man had been issued a K-ration for lunch, but at noon they were on the bomb run. And, who could eat a K-ration at fifty degrees below zero? So, off to the mess hall and the evening meal. Then, at six o'clock the Battle Order was posted. Thornton's crew was to fly again the next day. If they got off it would be the fourth day in a row that the 353rd lofted their bombers. When supper ended they each realized how tired they were—and how soon the 4 a.m. call would arrive. Sack time!

Exactly on schedule, the mournful voice of the sergeant who was the orderly gave the wake-up call. Those few who shaved had learned to get this chore out of the way the night before a mission. Seven hours with an oxygen mask clinging to a freshly shaved face can be some kind of torture. To the mess hall for a light breakfast and then to the briefing room.

When the target map was first displayed there were groans from all the crews as it looked like a repeat trip to Blechhammer. But the target was Odertal, Germany—a part of the Blechhammer complex but somewhat isolated. Interest heightened when it was learned that this small refinery was producing the jet fuel for the new very fast Me-262's. This target was not ringed with the same massive flak defenses as Blechhammer North—but well-defended nonetheless. The mission was almost a carbon copy of the one the day before. The Thornton crew was in the tail-end spot again. The skill of both pilots in formation flying was now very good. They brought the plane (Aircraft #284) into formation very smoothly. The plane is always brought in from below giving the pilots a continuous and clear view of the guidon plane (or wingman). The classic arrangement for a squadron consists of six planes, two sets of three each in a triangular pattern. The second set of three is to the right and below the leading three. A seventh plane in the "tail end" position would form a diamond pattern for the second unit, now with four planes. This formation of squadron planes headed NNE over the coast with its clear view of Termoli on the port side. Across the Adriatic the squadron came into formation with the other squadrons of the 301st Group at the rendezvous point, the island of Vis. There were only broken clouds below which gave them a good view for the rendezvous maneuver, a giant circle with Vis as the pylon. At different points on this circle each Squadron drops into place. The crew was a little less tense than they were yesterday and could enjoy more the view of the beautiful Adriatic, the many islands of the Dalmation coast of Yugoslavia and the snow-capped Andaric Mountains. Always climbing, they crossed over into Hungary, missing Nagykanitsa by a safe margin. Bass got another good look at Lake Balaton and a pilotage "fix" which confirmed they were on course and on schedule. Periodically they could see their "little friends," the fighter escorts. A familiar sight would be the Mustangs of the "checkered tail Squadron." The fighters from this squadron kept much closer to the bombers and were less prone to wander off looking for more excitement than accompanying the slow bombers. As they crossed into Czechoslovakia the cloud cover became almost solid again. But today the planes were developing beautiful contrails adding a dimension to the mystical beauty of the B-17 in this mighty armada. As they approached the IP they could see the planes in the squadrons ahead on the bomb run as they headed into the black puffs of Nazi flak.

Today there were more sweaty palms and sinking sensations than yesterday. But the bomb run was shorter, only six minutes, and there was heavy fire for only three minutes—long minutes. This was another day of MICKEY bombing, a frustration for Rury, who wanted to look through his Norden Sight and see a German target. All six following planes watched the lead plane. As soon as the lead plane bombs were visible each of the six bombardiers triggered his intervalometer to start bombs falling at one per second from each plane. Again the bomb load per plane was twelve 500-pound RDX high explosive bombs. Rury could see the shock waves in the clouds as the bombs from other planes exploded.

The gunners kept a close watch for enemy fighters but none showed. After Rury's "bombs away" they rallied to the right and assumed a homeward course with the noontime sun beaming dead ahead. It was almost the winter solstice and Odertal was at 50 degrees N latitude. The sun at high noon was only 17 degrees elevation. But they could shed their flak suits and pretend they were veterans now.

The further south they went the more they could relax even though they would be over German held territory until they crossed the Adriatic coast. The more successful they were in destroying the oil targets the less likelihood there was that enemy fighters would try to intercept them, especially after the bomb run. The sun through the Plexiglas nose warmed that section of the plane from minus fifty to minus ten degrees F—and Rury started to get sleepy. But his five-minute-apart oxygen checks would bring him back to the reality of the situation. On south they flew and the clouds started to dissipate. They were almost gleeful to see the rugged coast of Yugoslavia and the sparkling blue of the Adriatic. Even Bass could relax now, for the pilots could get "on the beam" and home right in to the Lucera airfield. There was less of a crosswind today and the formation landing was smooth as silk. The left plane "peels off" first and makes a tight 360 to head in to the landing strip. Each succeeding plane makes a slightly larger 360 and all seven planes land with about a minute interval between planes.

So it was debriefing, a shot of whiskey, coffee and doughnuts and smiles from the Red Cross ladies. None of this repetition was boring, however. As two-mission veterans the talk about the day's events was much more animated than the day before. They were still talking on the way to the mess hall where their hunger made even the C rations meal taste good. After supper they all headed for the bulletin board area and awaited the posting of the BO. Sure enough, Thornton and crew were on the schedule for December 20. It was back to the tents. Most of the tents by now had a makeshift stove that was gasoline fueled. Their one luxury was to heat water in their metal helmets and get a hot shave or even a hot shampoo. They were too tired to write letters that night—or read—or even talk about females. Sleep came early!

And so did the wakeup call. Most of them felt like they were in a daze until they hit the cold shower. How they yearned for a double dose of hot coffee, but the value of an empty bladder overruled this craving. The surprise at the mess hall was the treat of _fresh_ eggs. Two over easy hit the spot.

Now that they knew more about combat flying the trepidation level prior to briefing increased. They had more questions they could ask themselves. The one most frequently posed was "Which oil target would it be today?" The answer came all too soon, when the mission map was displayed on the screen. For the third day in a row you could see the target point right there near the "three corners of Poland, Germany and Czechoslovakia." It would be a repeat of their first mission—back to Blechhammer North. Even the name sounded tough. The literal translation is "hammer of tin." Mythology buff Bass insisted this might be the hammer of Thor. Thor was the Norse and Germanic god of thunder. He was the number one son of god number one, Odin. Thor carried a magical hammer against his enemies and the sparks from the hammer were the lightning flashes.

So, with Blechhammer as the day's target, they now knew exactly what the flak would be like. And, they also knew that

the German fighters had been put up only once in the last
month—to defend against their attempt to knock out
Blechhammer two days ago. This target was important to both
sides. The forecast for the weather implied that not much had
changed since yesterday. Scattered clouds over Italy and the
Adriatic should not impede the rendezvous, and clouds over the
target would mean MICKEY bombing.

Each of the crew went through his preflight check very intently. They waited in the plane on the hardstand only a short
while when the signal came to "execute Plan Able." Narracci
started each of the four engines and he and Thornton listened
for any telltale signs of trouble. Smooth as ever. They started to
taxi to the tail end Charlie spot while everyone who could see
watched the planes ahead on the takeoff pattern. There was
only a 45-second interval between planes. There would be one
plane just aloft past the end of the runway, a second plane accel-
erating at full throttle in the middle of the runway and a third
plane revving up to start on its way. With such a short interval
the "prop wash" from the preceding plane could often be more
than just a nuisance. Since Blechhammer was very distant, almost at the limit of the bombers' range, full fuel load was required. And, again the full bomb load, of twelve 500-pound RDX
bombs was aboard. The one time a B-17 felt "sloppy" was at takeoff with maximum load.

Both pilots worked hard on the rudder and surface controls
when they felt "prop wash." Rury, who wanted to be a pilot,
could now understand why the B-17 pilots were almost always
both tall and strong. And today these two strong pilots brought
their plane smoothly into squadron formation. They followed
their wingman into the rendezvous. Today the 353rd was the
high squadron, above, to the right, and to the rear of the lead
squadron.

It was cloudy most of the way and Bass was busy with his
Mercator map and his "dead reckoning" navigation. The wind
was the big unknown. Clouds made it difficult to measure the
"drift" of the plane and to determine an accurate ground speed.
He searched for a break when he was near Lake Balaton, hoping

to get a pilotage fix. No luck. So back to the calculations. Only the Group lead planes had radar navigational equipment aboard. Bass was forced to assume the lead planes were following the flight plan. It was almost 12:40 p.m. before they reached the IP. Lake and Taylor had dispensed all of the "chaff" several minutes before the bomb run. All the gunners strained to be the first to spot an enemy fighter. But none appeared. Once on the bomb run, Bass, Rury, Schratz and the two pilots had the best forward view. They all agreed that the flak was even heavier than two days ago. Most had donned the oppressive flak suits. Rury called that the bomb doors were open. With his finger on the toggle switch he watched for the sign of the first bomb from the lead plane. Each of the high squadron planes was to drop all twelve bombs together today. When Rury released this three tons of weight the plane lurched. With all the flak bursting about them some thought they had been hit. Not so! Again, they followed their wingman as the high squadron rallied to the right and into the low-hanging sun. Still no enemy fighters in sight. But the "red tails" or "checkered tails" of the escort Mustangs could be seen in the distance. These "red tails" always stuck to their job.

On the flight south there was little banter or joviality in the intercom exchanges. Each was musing and concluded that his tension level was higher on the second run over Blechhammer. And they were tired—not exhausted, but weary. The cloud cover obscured any spectacular views except for Yovich's view of the other bombers who were following them southward.

The right outboard engine was not maintaining manifold pressure properly and it sounded a little strange to Narracci. Schratz called to say that he could see a small oil leak behind the cowling. The motor became noisier and Thornton decided to "feather" the propeller. It is a strange feeling to look at a motor and see that stationary propeller. But the three engines took up the slack and they maintained formation position with no difficulty. They landed at Lucera with the engine still out. It was a three-point soft landing. Later the crew chief said there was a flak puncture in the engine—and about a dozen small flak holes in the right wing. At least one of those flak bursts had been close.

The plane that day was aircraft #429, the same plane they took to Blechhammer two days earlier.

The debriefing was more of a chore today. But, the whiskey tasted better and the coffee and doughnuts started a revival of spirits. They were sure it would be somebody else's flight tomorrow. They wolfed down the C rations converted to supper—and headed directly for the bulletin board. But they had to wait until 6 p.m. as always. When the BO was posted there was Thornton's crew again. Damn!

Thornton called the crew together and gave them a little pep talk and reminded them how pissed they were to be scratched from a BO just one week ago tonight. So, it was off to tent city and the two blankets and canvas cot. At least they were too tired to have nightmares.

They got an extra hour sleep because the wakeup call came at 5 a.m. Maybe the mission was to be postponed? But they got ready and headed for the briefing hut with thoughts of Blechhammer on the mind. There were sighs of relief when the target map was revealed. On display was a route directly into the heart of southern Germany : target = Oil at Regensburg. And the weatherman got a few cheers when he said that the front causing the bad weather over the targets for three days had moved to the southeast. The cloud cover over target would be minimal or nil. Rury and Bass were delighted to hear that they would be able to "see" on this mission. They were spirited as they headed for their plane—#429 again with a repaired engine and nearly invisible patches over the flak holes. The ground crew had swarmed all over the plane as soon as the engines stopped turning the day before. Schratz was with them for an hour at night and was on the flight line before the rest of the crew arrived. He was satisfied that 429 was ready. But Thornton gave it his eagle eye inspection too. In they climbed and awaited either the "go" or "abort" signal. It was go! They were to fly today off the left wing of the squadron lead plane. And the squadron would be in the "low" position in the group—to the left and below the lead squadron. The group was going into Regensburg alone, but a major effort with 29 planes scheduled. The rest of the Fifth Wing was heading for Vienna. The group rendezvous would be at Ancona, on the Italian Adriatic coast, up the boot leg from Lucera. They would have fighter escort from Venice to the target and return.

On this mission visibility was to be excellent, both up and back. First they flew over the Adriatic for 300 nautical miles. To the west they could observe the Appenine Mountains that form the spine of Italy extending from the toe of the "boot" to the magnificent Po valley that stretches across the leg from Genoa to Venice. North of the Po valley are the great mountain ranges. From Mt. Blanc in France the mountain grandeur of the Alps forms a great arc encompassing Switzerland, southern Germany and Austria—with the lesser Alps continuing the arc into Yugoslavia. This Alpen arc was like a section of a circle with Lucera, the 353rd base, as the center.

The squadron joined the group at Ancona and picked up the "red tail" Mustang escort planes at the north end of the Adriatic. Bass pointed out the spidery shape that was Venice several miles to the west.

They were at 10,000 feet as they passed Venice. Rury signaled to go on oxygen. Dead ahead loomed the awesome sight of the snow-covered Alpen peaks, a few rising to almost their flight altitude. But ever higher they climbed. From the air these rugged, jagged peaks look soft and marshmallowy. Buckel described them best—as a cake with a thick, smooth, creamy-white frosting.

They passed the Dolomites and then Brenner Pass. They were a comfortable 20 miles from the Pass, where the Germans had installed Flak guns at 6000 feet. An unwary plane, even at 12,000 feet was a sitting duck if it strayed over the Brenner gunners. They passed Innsbruck and could see the powerful Zugspitz, the highest mountain in Germany—towering to over 10,000 feet. North of the Zugspitz the ground elevation dropped rapidly as the great Danube plain stretched out in front of them.

The Danube River starts east of Basel and stretches almost due east through Regensburg to Vienna and Budapest—thence south through the Great Hungarian Plain to Belgrade and once again eastward, ever eastward to its multiple mouths in the Black Sea.

For the first time the crew saw a major city in Germany as they slipped by Munich on a direct line for the IP, Ingolstadt. Ingolstadt lies about a mile south of the Danube and forty miles from the target, the oil refinery near Regensburg. The target was on the river shore at the confluence with one of the Danube tributaries. Bass and Rury conferred and agreed on the positive identification. Rury scanned upriver from the target and could identify the aiming point. Before they arrived at the aiming point they were in, as Buckel said, a pack of flak. Rury picked out another aiming point about a minute up river from the real one and practiced picking it up on his Norden. He yearned to sight and drop the bombs himself, but the orders were to toggle the entire load when the lead plane showed its falling bombs. Rury did this and the plane gave that little lurch. Thornton immediately started evasive action as he readied to rally to the right. Rury had given Yovich a special briefing on the location of the target. So Hap could easily pick out this "Y" in the rivers and he kept his eye on the area. It looked like a lot of direct hits and a few huge pillars of smoke were boiling upward as Yovich watched the target recede in the distance. This was the first time that the crew had been able to see their results and the sense of exhilaration offset the earlier queasy feelings in the gut they had experienced on the bomb run.

Once again the 301st had "done good" and the twenty-nine planes headed south in perfect formation. The gunners swept the skies for signs of interceptors with a mixture of apprehension and hope for the challenge. As he always did, Schratz kept spinning his top turret. From this vantage point he could see in all directions and fire his twin fifties in all directions except directly rearward, a mechanical restriction that prevented top gunners from shooting their own tail.

By the time they left enemy territory and were over the Adriatic, a real sense of weariness enveloped them all. Four missions in four days. They felt like veterans. What they weren't aware of was the frenzy at 15th headquarters to take advantage of the recent good weather and launch maximum effort against the oil targets. For off to the north the German Panzer units were taking advantage of the miserable flying weather over

France and Belgium to counterattack through the Ardennes in what we now call the "Battle of the Bulge." It was up to the 15th to help shut down this German armor.

The trip back was uneventful, but there was more verve to the chatter. They knew they had hit the refinery hard, and they would have evidence today. At the Adriatic east of Venice one of the planes in the squadron which had carried the photographer broke from formation and headed for home at full speed. The photographer was a big sergeant of Greek ancestry, Sgt. Andropoulous. He was a big husky guy who wore a small flak suit shaped like a Greek soldier's skirt. He had been hit in the ass by shrapnel on his first mission and wanted to avoid that repeat.

The rest of the planes came home and landed per the SOP. There were more extensive debriefing sessions because of the clear weather. Rury was also told to attend a bombardier's review at 6:30 p.m. when the photographs of the target before, during and after the bombing would be shown.

After the perfunctory trip to the mess hall they gathered by the bulletin board. Surely they would have a stand down after four in four days—almost a record for a new crew. But when the BO was posted there was Thornton and crew. Only Taylor would get to sleep. Thornton's plane would be the photography plane and Andropoulous would take the place of Taylor in the waist. Rury headed for the bombardier critique. Later he could report that the damage to the distillation towers and hydrogenation unit was virtually irreparable. There would be no synthetic oil made at Regensburg for quite a while.

When the mournful sergeant called them over the PA the next morning they rolled out of the sack at 4:30 and it seemed colder, wetter, and foggier than usual. Or was that their spirits? They went to roll call, ate a pancake breakfast and then made the muddy hike to the briefing hut.

When the target and route map were displayed they knew it would be a long and tough run. The target was the other Big B. The largest synthetic oil refinery was at Brux. The two big B's were Brux and Blechhammer—often referred to in one mouthful as if they were one target. Brux was even further from Lucera than Blechhammer. It would take all the fuel the B-17's

Another Oil Target.

B-17 and a "little friend."

could hold. But even before the briefing had been completed word came down from headquarters that the mission had been scrubbed. The drizzly foggy weather had socked-in not only the Fifth Wing but the fighter escort which would make up the assault planned against Brux that day.

Before he dismissed the weary crews, Major Paine read a congratulatory message from General Ira C. Eaker, Commanding General of the Mediterranean Allied Air Forces. He stated that despite the poor weather the 15th had dispatched over 1,000 bombers per day on each of the previous six days, a record. All of the sorties in this steady assault were against enemy oil installations.

A few hours of sack time were in order. How refreshed they felt after the naps and a chance to quaff three or even four cups of coffee. They were still feeling warm and fuzzy from having witnessed the direct strikes and the burning target on yesterday's raid. There was time in the afternoon for a few mundane activities, like fixing up their tent areas or taking their laundry in to Lucera. All the Italian mothers in the village were glad to make a little money by taking in laundry. However, Bass made the mistake of taking some candy with him to give to children who looked so peaked and hungry. As soon as he had given away the second piece a mob of both kids and adults swarmed all over him. He dropped the bag of goodies and fled.

You can bet that all errands were complete by late afternoon. Everybody was in the bulletin area when the BO was posted at six. Thornton's crew, except for Taylor, were scheduled for tomorrow, December 22. That meant early call for the sixth consecutive day. Despite the naps, most hit the sack early and slept soundly.

But 4:30 a.m. is early for rising. And there were yawns and stretches galore. Like automatons they went through the paces of dressing and eating and trekking through the mud to the briefing hall. The weather was miserable but this day they displayed an honest ambivalence about bad weather. They could use another stand down. The briefing went forward. Again the target was Brux. But the briefing ended early when, like yesterday, headquarters scrubbed flying for that day.

As an airplane commander who had flown four missions in four days Thornton had enough pull to be able to get a squadron jeep for the rest of the day. He rounded up a few of the enlisted men and they headed in to Foggia, about 15 miles to the east and much larger than Lucera. But the stores in Foggia were virtually empty. Here they were getting both flight pay and combat pay, and there was nothing to buy. They had been warned against buying and eating local foods. But occasionally they would find an outside market where a few fresh fruits were available. Oranges were always safe. And there was a USO building in Foggia. That afternoon they saw an excellent movie. It was John Ford's production of "Stagecoach," not a new movie, but already a "classic."

On the way back, both Scott and Buckel expressed concern that being scheduled for Brux for two days in a row was an item that German Intelligence might somehow pick up. They were that good. Scott said he half expected to hear Axis Sally say in her next broadcast "Welcome 301st to Brux, we are waiting for you!" Thornton said he would relay this concern to the G2 briefing officer.

The crew gathered at the bulletin board well before 6. Bass pointed out an interesting feature of the big B's, Brux and Blechhammer. They each formed an anchor of the Sudetenland, Brux at the west corner and Blechhammer at the east. It was here that the WWII really started. It was in Munich in 1938 that the French and British kowtowed to Hitler, with the head-in-the-sand acquiescence of the U.S. This shameful appeasement ceded to Germany that part of Czechoslovakia along the German border called Sudetenland. It is a land rich in minerals with vast deposits of coal. All of the Czech border defenses against the Germans were in the Sudetes Mountains. With those gone the Germans occupied all of the country at will. After he had won this major first battle of the war Hitler abandoned any pretenses and got ready to invade Poland the following year. So it was only fitting that Hitler would suffer a major defeat by the Fifth Wing here in the Sudetes. Remember the strategy of the Fifteenth—"gridlock the mighty Nazi war machine by denying it oil."

Enough of philosophy. At 6 they could read the names on the BO. Thornton and his crew, less Taylor, were listed. But the next morning for the third time, while being briefed on a mission to Brux, the mission was scrubbed. They spent part of this December 23 trying to make the tents a little more festive. Thornton's wife had sent him a Christmas present, on his request, that consisted of a dozen light bulbs. The tents had one electrical outlet each, but Supply had no light bulbs. Thornton made presents of these bulbs and Lake unearthed a large clump of "chaff." There was tinsel galore—and a little light. Before six they gathered at their "Mecca." Scott got the biggest laugh when he said "Surely they wouldn't make us fly on Christmas Eve." But there they were on the BO for December 24.

The weather in the Lucera area looked much more promising the next morning—no drizzle and no fog. It was a full briefing that morning. All six groups of the Fifth Wing were to hit the target at Brux. The crew gathered all of their personal gear and rode by truck through the mud to the planes. They waited. And they waited. After two hours up went the red flare—mission scrubbed.

They lolled around the tent area most of the day. They had sent out their Christmas cards long ago, but this was a good day for writing letters. The letters had to be censored. The officers' letters by the adjutant and the enlisted men's letters by one of the crew officers. Scott was the only one who would not let his crew officers read his mail. He took his letters to the adjutant office for censorship. They had all learned that the safest way to talk about specific missions they had been on was to enclose a clipping from the "Stars and Stripes" Army newspaper—or to make a direct quote from this source. And once again they gathered before six to await the BO. Scott didn't make the mistake of saying "Surely they wouldn't fly us on Christmas." Good thing too, because for the ninth consecutive day they had BO. At least they weren't sleepy now. Almost all of them decided to go to the little building the chaplain called the church. Darkness came early this Christmas Eve. One of the fliers sat down at the portable organ and started pumping out carols. It was hauntingly strange to be singing "...sleep in Heavenly peace" in their battle clothes. To the north the Luftwaffe and the flak gunners were singing "...schlaff im Himmlischer Ruh."

They slept, but fitfully rather than peacefully, and they awoke early on this birth of Jesus day. A few smiles replaced the grim countenances when they found there were fresh eggs this morning. The corporal on KP was frying them to order—two to a flier... ah joy to the world! To the briefing hut. It was dark, of course, but you could see that the target would be Brux—but to a man they were sure the Jerries knew this too. The pilots listened intently to the weatherman. He assured them that this somewhat soupy condition would clear once they were over the Adriatic, only thirty miles away. He forecast broken clouds enroute and solid overcast over the target. And he was right all the way. Thornton was flying second, off the right wing of the Squadron Lead, a good spot for this low visibility takeoff. The plane intervals were a minute apart today and the procedure was for each successive plane to maintain 100 feet of space with the plane ahead and to fly in trail formation north to the Adriatic. Major Paine stressed the absolute necessity that a plane not lose sight of its guidon (wingman).

They already knew that this was a helluva long mission—at the fringe of the range of the Flying Forts. In fact, the Liberators were going to a closer but tough oil target in Vienna. Actually, the B-24 Liberator had a longer range than the B-17 at low altitude, but not at high altitude and full load. Paine told each pilot to review ditching procedures before boarding the plane. He pointed out that there was a smooth beach area just north of Lake Lessina, in case a plane did not have enough fuel for the last thirty miles to Lucera. You could tell he was expecting some planes would run out of fuel. This, surprisingly enough, usually happened if planes were forced to fly with three—or even two engines. He concluded by saying he thought this Christmas mission would rank as one of the most important missions the Fifth Wing ever flew.

So it was off to the planes in the soupy weather. Everybody expected to see the red flare after they boarded the planes. But the crew was in their plane, # 8500, only fifteen minutes when the order to "Execute Plan Able" was received. Thornton followed the lead plane, kept his 100 foot distance and his eyes on the plane ahead, as they headed north through the soup. In twenty minutes the weather cleared and the planes started to drop into their assigned formation positions as they headed for Ancona. There they made rendezvous with the other squadrons. The 353rd was in the high squadron position today. Up ahead they could see the Forts of the 97th Group, which was leading the Fifth Wing, as it had done so often on important missions. Of the hundred groups in the entire European area the 97th was the only group that had flown more missions (and only a few) than the 301st. More on that later.

They headed NNE up the Adriatic crossing the coast just east of Venice, then straight north crossing the Carnic Alps at the border of Italy and Austria, north across the mighty Austrian Alps, past Hitler's retreat at Berchtesgaden and the Austrian city of Salzburg, across the tip of the southeastern section of Germany and the Danube River, then straight north across the western part of Czechoslovakia. The cloud cover was intensifying as they went north. The last positive navigational fix was when the squadron crossed the Danube. This permitted Bass to calculate the ground speed exactly and determine a precise ETA for the IP, Rittersgrun. Bass could hardly believe his eyes when the group lead plane overshot the IP by two minutes. The lead plane then tried to correct the course toward the target. The 353rd had no choice but to follow the leader. The flak over Brux was the heaviest they had seen. About three minutes from target a burst dead ahead sent shrapnel directly at the nose. This time Bass and Rury could hear the burst and see the two tiny holes appear in the Plexiglas plane front and hear the spent flak rattle inside the compartment. No injury though.

Rury had his eyes glued on the lead plane as they approached the aiming point. But the lead bombardier had been confused by his navigator's error at the IP. In any case, he didn't drop his bombs! Consequently, no one in the group bombed. Then the lead plane rallied left (instead of to the right). Thornton knew immediately that the colonel was going to take them around again. Twenty-nine crews soon knew this too.

Never was a man so profaned in a ten minute period than was the Colonel. His ancestry and that of his mother were questioned. His legitimacy was denied. He was reviled in the coarsest terms. He was accused of indulging in every bizarre and sordid sexual perversion known to fliers—and some they made up... but deep down each flier of the 301st who would face his second bomb run that hour was also saying that the "old man has balls!" This 360 over Brux on Christmas Day was to add another fine chapter to the history of the legendary 301st.

The worst part was the fact they had used up most of their "reserve" on the first bomb run. Later each of the ten on Thornton's plane admitted he was scared that morning. But the second pass was easier. The surprise move had confused the flak gunners too. The lead plane got a firm lock on the aiming point this time. Rury toggled his bombs with split second timing. They could see the massive shock waves ripple through the cloud layer. Andropoulous could not get good pictures of the target. But he photographed the flak patterns, got three pictures of a disabled plane as it pulled out of formation, and of course had a photographic record of the snafu on the first run.

After "bombs away" the squadron rallied to the right and headed southward. There were a few muted prayers of thanks offered, even as they scanned the skies for interceptors. After the wave of relief Thornton got on the intercom to remind them "you really earned an Air Medal today." It was their fifth mission (six bomb runs), the mission quota set to receive this award.

With a little tail wind they moved right along. The clouds started to break in time for them to see the spectacular vision of the Alps, with a few of the peaks visible above the cloud cover. At the Adriatic, with 300 miles to go, their plane could leave formation and steam for Lucera at full speed, but keeping an eye on the fuel gages. Naturally they were the first home with the day's photographs. They had their Christmas glass of cheer and, after debriefing, hit the chow line. It was their first real meal since arriving at the 353rd. The Christmas turkey and trimmings hit the spot—after eight hours of flying and twelve without food. It was a memorable meal on a memorable day. And, at 6 they received a Christmas present. They were not on the BO for the first time in ten days! Now they could appreciate just how fagged-out they were. But they knew they could sleep right through breakfast tomorrow. The next day they got a better Christmas Day present. Rury was called for a special bombardier's critique. A recon plane had skipped in over Brux below the clouds to get a set of photos. The analysis showed that Brux was utterly destroyed. There would be no more planes lost over Brux. (Note: Even the name Brux has been destroyed. After the war this strip of Germany was ceded to Czechoslovakia and Brux is now called Most.)

With Brux destroyed Headquarters pledged to get the other Big B, Blechhammer. They did this on December 28.

Thornton's crew had a two-day stand down, which they enjoyed as they relaxed and rested. But the 6 p.m. BO on the 27th included their names.

The briefing the next morning seemed like a broken record. They always got a sinking feeling when the name Blechhammer appeared as the target. Bass and the pilots now knew much about the route to this target. But familiarity here bred no contempt—only respect.

The weather forecast was for clear weather over the target and over much of the route. This made the navigation and bombing easier, but boded ill for the barrage of defensive fire they would meet. After the jeep rides to their plane, they found it would be old #429 again. Taylor said that the plane ought to belong to them so they could name it. Scott suggested "The Blechhammer Express." Buckel said that after listening to Bass that his choice would be "Thor's Hammer." He could picture a sketch of this Norse god striking a blow with the lightning flashing from his hammer. Thornton and the others liked that too.

The takeoff and squadron formation was smooth. The group rendezvous was over Vis and the Wing now headed NNE toward Blechhammer. The group went directly over Lake Balaton. It crossed the Danube about midway between Vienna and Budapest. At this point Bass pointed out the higher mountains of the Alps off to the west. North of the Danube the course paralleled the valley of the Vah, a major tributary of the

Danube. As the group flew up this valley the Little Carpathian and White Carpathian Mountains were visible on the left. To the east the grandeur of the main Carpathian Range rivaled the Alps in majesty. Like the Alps, the Carpathians form a huge arc. This arc extends along the Czech and Polish border and curves southward into Romania, ending in a scorpion tail shaped-hook called the Transylvanian Alps.

With the clear weather Bass could see the IP well before the lead plane arrived. He was certain the group would be there exactly on schedule. And, on schedule the group headed down the bomb run toward the fearsome Blechhammer. Thornton reminded them to don flak suits. Buckel realized his was just behind the radio compartment by the waist gunners. He clipped on a small oxygen tank and retrieved his flak suit and got help from Lake in putting it on. Just then there was a very close burst left of the plane. Several pieces of shrapnel pierced the fuselage. And one of these went between the front and back segments of Buckel's flak suit and directly into his heart. He died instantly. Lake caught him as he fell and realized in short order that any first aid was futile. Taylor got on the intercom to alert the crew and add to the already tense mind sets. Rury was able to see that the lead plane was coming right in on the aiming point and was certain when he toggled the release of the twelve five hundred pounders that the bombs would hit close to the refinery distillation towers. He could see the red and black flash of the bombs from earlier planes verifying that they had hit close to target also. He almost screamed "Bombs Away" as #429 lurched upward. Thornton followed his wingman as the planes rallied right and resumed evasive action flying patterns again. Narracci went back to the waist and confirmed that Buckel was dead.

Thornton told him to get back quickly because the #2 engine was losing oil pressure. It was beginning to vibrate too, obviously a consequence of the close flak burst. Thornton told Narracci to feather #2 while it still had oil pressure. Narracci went through the feathering procedure, making sure first it was #2 he was feathering. It came to a full feathered position—and then it began to unfeather. Narracci immediately pulled out the feathering switch for a few seconds and closed it. The prop feathered again and he pulled out the switch button again and all was O.K. Both pilots were well aware of the hazard of a "windmilling" propeller, so they breathed easier.

It was a disconsolate and long trip home despite the warming rays of the noontime sun. Thornton was told to land at Lucera as the first plane. An ambulance met them at the end of the landing strip and helped remove Buckel's body. Buckel, the tenth man, was buried in Italy in a quiet and somber ceremony. The Air Medal he had won but had never seen was on his uniform. This silent hero was draped in the flag he had served so willingly. He had known that the Fifth Wing had knocked out Brux. He did not know that the Wing had destroyed Blechhammer the day he died. The Big B's were dead too.

Now Sgt. George Marich became the tenth man and new radio operator. He joined the crew but it was to take awhile for him to become a member of the team. The crew was not scheduled for the next mission, which proved to be the last in 1944. The cold, wet, foggy, drizzly weather settled in with a vengeance. There was the hint that the drizzle would turn to snow. Each day there would be a BO posted—and a briefing would occur the next morning. The crews would trek to the planes, get ready and then wait—for the red flare. This charade was repeated the next day. The only real excitement was on New Year's Eve. After a lot of gin and scotch some too-happy fliers started fireworks with the 45 automatics they always carried on missions. And it snowed on New Year's Day. Finally the squadron sent the planes aloft on January 2, 1945 for the first mission of the year.

Thornton's crew were not on this first mission but were scheduled for January 3 and the mission was scrubbed. They were on again for the 4th and this time they flew. At the briefing it appeared that this might be their first "easy" mission. Major Paine said this would be the 400th mission flown by the 301st. It was a short run—up to Innsbruck in Austria. Material of war flowed south from Germany through Innsbruck and the Brenner Pass to the Po valley of Italy. There it was dispensed to German troops who were holding back the northward advance of the U.S. Fifth Army. Even the combat fliers admitted that the Fifth Army Infantry were battling tougher Germans on the ground than the 15th met in the air. The 15th was pledged to help.

Well... everything seemed to go wrong. There was a strong wind that morning, but fortunately not a crosswind. Thornton's plane was the sixth in the takeoff position—taking off to the west. The planes had a full bomb load and a little less than maximum fuel. But the strong wind meant that the plane's ground speed was very slow. West of the base was the village of Lucera, which was on a hill—not a high hill, but a hill nevertheless. And at the highest point stood the Lucera Castle.

Each time that Thornton and Narracci tried to gain altitude they would encounter "prop wash," a series of tiny invisible tornados created by the tips of the wings of planes ahead of them. So the vertical distance to the ground kept shrinking. They were "buzzing" with a full bomb load. It was terrifying for the crew. Bass turned his back to the nose and was transfixed by the frantic motion of the four gigantic boots on the feet of the pilots playing a concerto on the rudder pedals as they strove to gain a little altitude. The waist gunners were looking up at Lucera Castle. Lake asked Taylor to hand him his chute. Taciturn Texan Taylor simply said "That won't he'p you now!" It took every ounce of the pilots' skill and savvy to get that plane aloft. It was worse than a bomb run.

But they made formation and the rendezvous at Ancona. The cloud cover became more and more extensive. Bass wanted to get a good measure of the plane's drift while he could still see the ground. He couldn't believe the reading. But, you could look down and tell. They were heading northwest but the plane was going north, a drift of 45 degrees. He calculated the wind to be 110 knots out of the west. They kept climbing and kept seeing the cloud cover increase. What none of the navigators detected was that the wind was shifting very rapidly as altitude was gained. The wind direction was now out of the east. They were blown right over Brenner Pass. Suddenly there were a few unexpected flak bursts. A plane in the follow squadron was hit. Yovich screeched "B-17 going down... B-17 going down!" Only three parachutes were seen. By the time the ETA to the IP expired Bass was hopelessly lost. So was the lead navigator. They never found the target. As the cloud cover diminished Bass searched frantically for a pilotage fix. His eyes darted from the ground to his maps over and over. After ten minutes he spotted a huge lake. It was so big that there was only one possibility. It must be the Bodensee (Lake Constance). They were almost 100 miles off course... to the west. The lead navigator had figured this out too and headed south. This took them over the eastern tip of Switzerland—an incursion that was the strictest of no-no's. On the south course Bass could get a drift reading that confirmed the fantastic wind shift. Holding at this higher altitude the Group Lead took them to their secondary target, the marshalling yards in Verona, Italy—the city of Romeo and Juliet. Verona is north of the Po but on the Adige river and was easy to identify now that the clouds had dissipated. They hit the IP and went on the run to the aiming point and bombed visually. Flak was light and the bombing was accurate, a reasonable finish to a screwed-up mission. They headed down the Po valley and made the mistake of getting too close to Venice so took some more flak that should have been avoided. Once over the Adriatic they could relax and coast on in to the home base at Lucera. The interrogation for this short mission took longer than for the other missions to the critical oil targets. You can bet there was a lot of "ass chewing" that afternoon.

With the destruction of three of the four great synthetic oil plants—those at Regensburg, Brux and Blechhammer—only one remained, the unit at Ruhland, near Berlin, which was outside of the range of the heavy bombers from Italy. But there were about a dozen smaller refineries which were viable targets. Five of these smaller refineries were in the Vienna area and two were near Vienna—at Moosbierbaum and at Wiener-Neustadt. There was another in Austria, also on the Danube in a city named Linz. This would be the target for the crew's eighth mission.

The BO was posted on January 7, and the mission was January 8. This was the second screwed-up mission in a row. Let's blame this one on the weather. Conditions at Lucera were good and the squadron took off and made formation on schedule.

The cloud cover became solid over the Adriatic. Rendezvous was over the now invisible island of Vis and the 353rd was in the low position. The group left Vis on a heading of 350 degrees and while climbing encountered a second layer of clouds. With such poor visibility the 353rd lost contact and began to slow a little and stay even lower to prevent disaster. Once above the clouds the other group planes were nowhere to be seen. The 353rd was alone—and the squadron lead had no PFF or radar equipment. It was dead reckoning all the way. The squadron bombed on the ETA at target—not very satisfactory and reminiscent of the RAF night bombing technique.

The Italian weather was worse in January than in December. Fortunately Thornton's crew was not scheduled because there was a BO every night and a briefing every morning, followed by a scrubbed mission. So it would be almost two weeks before mission nine. After a mission was scrubbed the crew was free for the day. There were the obligatory ditching practice sessions and a lot of skeet shooting to keep the gunners sharp. But everybody hitchhiked to Foggia most days. There was one excellent movie shown. It was called "None But the Lonely Heart." Cary Grant played a most unusual role for him, maybe his best role ever—and Ethel Barrymore was at her exceptional best. The USO Players put on the Noel Coward play, "Private Lives," and very good it was.

In Foggia Bass was surprised to see quite a few black lieutenants and captains. He was a Southerner, but a very tolerant person, so had no problem with this situation. All of these young officers wore pilot wings. It turned out there was a whole squadron of blacks who were P-51 Mustang pilots. And guess what? They flew the planes with the red checkered tails—the pilots who did the very best job of flying escort for the B-17's. These pilots were well-educated, very articulate and many had learned to speak Italian. They were a product of Tuskegee Institute. Bass had cause to be respectful.

It would be the 19th of January before the weather would permit the crew to fly mission 9. The target was Brod, Yugoslavia. In the briefing the increasing importance of the secondary strategy of the Fifteenth was stressed. The Russians had launched a massive New Year's offensive all along the German eastern front. They were pushing west from Romania toward Yugoslavia. In addition there were thousands of Yugoslavs fighting in the hills against the hated Nazis. The Germans controlled only the cities and the transportation networks in Yugoslavia. The plan was to hit the transportation networks. But for the third mission in a row, everything seemed to go wrong. And it wasn't the weather this time.

The distance to Brod was less than half the distance to Brux, so it was a short mission. The bomb run was visual. Rury had the target spotted all the way. The flak was light but extremely accurate. The holes formed by the shrapnel were visible as well as audible. And, the lead plane did not drop bombs. Rury almost wept. For one thing he had activated the delayed action bombs which the plane carried that day. These had to be dumped in the Adriatic on the way home. Because Yugoslavia was an occupied country the orders were strict not to bomb indiscriminately. Positive identification by both navigator and bombardier of an approved target was required.

Thornton was furious. In the debriefing he protested that his crew should have been flying lead that day. Later the crew chief told him that he had counted fifty flak holes in the plane—and for what? Major Paine was furious too. He had a closed door session with the lead crew officers. And he ordered those crews to fly practice bomb runs at every chance available.

Even though the great refinery at Regensburg had been destroyed there were three large oil storage depots in that city. One of these was the target on January 20. The weather over Italy was O.K. but cloud cover was solid over the Alps and Germany, so it was a Mickey or "blind bombing" mission. Rury hated these, figuring that he could have stayed at home and let Bass toggle the bombs. Besides, there was no direct "feedback" about whether the target was hit. It was sometimes days before recon planes would get photos of the target area. But there was direct feedback from the anti-aircraft gunners—for the second mission in a row the plane came back peppered with holes. They all remembered how cleanly one of these pieces of shrapnel had snuffed the life of Buckel.

The miserable Italian weather continued and there were no more missions flown in January—not a good month. February started better. The crew flew on the first day. After the last eleven days of January spent suiting up and briefing they would finally get to fly. Italy in winter! What a place to fight an Air War! The plane on February 1 was #8164 and the target was Moosbierbaum, near Vienna. This was the third successive mission with very heavy flak. Moosbierbaum was another oil target and the Jerries were getting desperate for oil. They were bringing every gun they had to protect the diminishing number of oil targets. They stripped the defenses of Dresden, a city with no industry. They brought these guns to Ruhland and to Vienna. The 15th's stranglehold on oil had its own reward. The Luftwaffe was almost invisible.

The weather enroute was very good and Bass had a field day navigating. He hit his ETA to all the checkpoints and the IP. The bomb run was reminiscent of Blechhammer. A burst near the right side and close to the plane disabled the #2 engine. Narracci feathered the prop and #8164 sailed home on three. They loved that big-assed bird.

On February 2 those from Punxsutawney proclaimed Groundhog Day. It was cloudy in Lucera, a groundhog's harbinger of an early spring. Thornton received his promotion to first lieutenant and he and the crew flew a few practice bomb runs, both signals that a squadron lead was near. But there was another weather-induced hiatus. For two weeks it was cold, damp and foggy. They flew no missions. It was a time for letter writing, visits to town, laundry, haircuts, and midnight snacks cooked on the oil drum stove.

On Valentine's Day the crew headed north on mission #12 in Aircraft #6666. It was a very rough mission for the squadron. One plane went down but the flak missed #6666. The target was in Vienna, the capital of Austria. The specific target was a small refinery in the north sector. Even from five miles up, Vienna is a beautiful city. The Danube makes a gentle S turn as it flows into and ebbs away from the city. The target was partially obscured by a smoke screen but the group and the squadron did well.

Valentine's Day was the second anniversary of the first bombing mission flown by the Fifth Wing. But the 301st was even older. Here is a brief history:

In the first six months after Pearl Harbor all of the combat B-17's were in the Pacific. By June 1942 there were two groups about ready for combat in Europe—the 97th and 301st. Their orders to Europe were delayed for a few weeks until the Battle of Midway results were well known. This first victory over the Japanese signaled the strength of the Naval Air arm. So the B-17's were consigned to Europe—and were stationed in England at Prestwick. The first B-17 arrived at Prestwick on July 1. This was the beginning of the buildup of the famed Eighth Air Force under the leadership of General Ira C. Eaker.

The RAF had been flying heavy bombers over German territory for two years—but always at night. Radar or PFF bombing was not yet developed so the RAF used pattern bombing of large targets—often with thousands of incendiary bombs. The Eighth was determined to fly in daylight and go after specific strategic targets. For this they needed fighter escort to help fend off the skilled veteran fighter pilots of the Luftwaffe. At this time there were no long range fighters, so this limited the range of the B-17's at first. The first raid was made by the 97th Group on August 17, 1942—sending just 12 planes to bomb railroads in Rouen, France. This raid was led by General Eaker, himself. On September 5 the 97th returned to Rouen accompanied by the 301st on the latter group's first mission. These two groups started the Eighth and were its nucleus as it grew. But not for long would they be in the Eighth. On November 5 six planes of the 97th flew an unusual mission—from England to Gibraltar. The flight was led by Maj. Paul Tibbets, who later gained fame by ending the war with Japan while flying the Enola Gay. Aboard these six planes were such famed army personnel as Generals Eisenhower, Mark Clark and James Doolittle. Eisenhower would use Gibraltar for his headquarters as Supreme Commander for the Invasion of North Africa.

The legendary Doolittle, the bomber of Tokyo, was named Commanding General of a new Air Force, the Twelfth, which would be stationed in North Africa. The now-veteran 97th and

Contrails over Germany.

Over Vienna.

301st Groups were transferred from the Eighth to become the Fifth Wing and nucleus of this new Air Force. After the successful invasion, the Fifth Wing was stationed at Biskra, near Oran—a city familiar to Thornton's crew. The Fifth Wing (consisting then of only the two groups) flew its first combat mission on Valentine's Day, 1943. The targets were docks and shipping at the Tunisian ports of Sfax and Sousse.

In the months to come the Wing participated in support of the infantry as Patton from the west and Montgomery from the east destroyed the once-vaunted Nazi *Afrika Korps.* In May 1943 the Wing pummeled the island of Pantelleria—so successfully that the island surrendered to the first infantry soldier to "hit the beach." They supported the invasion and occupation of Sicily and the invasion of Italy. Several times they bombed German airfields in the Foggia area not knowing then their own future there.

The 97th and 301st had started the 8th Air Force and the 12th Air Force. They were to start another. On November 1, 1943 the 15th Air Force was born. The 12th was dissolved and Doolittle became the first head of the 15th. By 1944 the Fifth Wing B-17's were stationed in various sectors near their former target of Foggia. Early in 1944 there were some key personnel shifts. General Eaker, of the Eighth, was promoted to a new position—commanding the Mediterranean Allied Air Forces (RAF as well as American). Doolittle was transferred to head the 8th and General Twining became head of the 15th.

The Fifth Wing's anniversary mission to Vienna was the 450th mission in the two years. Only 520 B-17's were lost in this two-year period. General Eaker commended the Wing on its record and especially on the "Mickey bombing destruction of Brux on Christmas Day." He added that "the 15th AF is undoubtedly the leading exponent in the world today of blind bombing."

During the debriefing of the Vienna mission Thornton was told that his crew would be flying squadron lead from then on. But first things first. After 12 missions a crew was "ordered" to take ten days rest leave. These ten combat fliers headed off, by one's, two's and three's, to Naples, to Capri, to Rome—the nouveau tourists—and ten glorious days of no shooting. They luxuriated in that and in the splendor of the hotels, especially in Capri. All during this leave Bass had been giving thought to the lead crew assignment. The upshot was the he told Thornton he did not want the responsibility of lead navigator. Thornton was nonplused because he considered Bass his most capable crew member. But he heeded his navigator's wishes. And, Lt. Tyler became the tenth man. Tyler had flown each of the missions Thornton had—except the last Blechhammer mission. Tyler had flown as navigator with half a dozen other pilots and came well recommended. Thornton and crew were dubious.

The first lead mission was their thirteenth on the 1st of March in Aircraft #184. Triskaidekaphobia is respected by all who fly. Fortunately the target was Maribor in Yugoslavia. Till now Maribor had not been a target so was less heavily defended. It is located just south of the Austrian border and due west of Lake Balaton. The Germans were mounting a counterattack against the Russians who were now at the gates of Budapest. Maribor was the funnel through which poured the German supplies for the counterattack. Tyler's navigation on this mission was not up to the excellence that Bass had displayed. The crew was still dubious. In any case there were more than a few thankful prayers uttered to have #13 behind them.

Mission #14 was flown on March 4 in Aircraft #6384. The 353rd was flying as the low squadron that day. Tyler's tentmate, Lt. Dutton, was group lead navigator and the target was the railroad center in Zagreb, Yugoslavia. Just before the group arrived at the IP Thornton's plane developed engine trouble and could not keep up with the group. Thornton decided to bomb the nearest "target of opportunity," which Tyler identified as Graz, Austria. Rury picked out a bridge and railroad yards and the 353rd went on this bomb run alone. All went well and Thornton's plane limped home with the rest of the Squadron following at the slow pace.

The rest of the group hit heavy fire over Zagreb and Dutton's plane was forced to "ditch" in the Adriatic. Dutton and two others on that group lead plane drowned that day.

They flew mission #15 on March 8. The target was the railroad complex in Hegyeshalom, Hungary. It was a relatively small target so the 353rd went alone. The weather was excellent. The target was only 70 miles from the Russian front. By knocking out the rail lines the Fifteenth could deny the Germans, already short of oil, the transport necessary to halt the Russian advance. Tyler's navigation was his best yet. He helped Rury identify the target as they crossed the IP. In all the occupied countries, like Hungary, it was required that the navigator and bombardier have positive identification of target before bombing. Rury put that Norden Bombsight to good use that day. The bombs fell dead center. Thornton rallied right and headed southwest past the familiar Lake Balaton, across Yugoslavia, across the Adriatic and home. The crew was elated at this success at lead. Thornton told them that they deserved their second Air Medals, which they had earned for fifteen missions. That day Tyler joined the team. Also, he was notified that he was now a first lieutenant—after eighteen months as a shavetail.

The next two missions were crazy. The crew got credit for the first—and probably should not have—and didn't get credit for the next, when maybe they should have. What goes around comes around!

Mission #16 was on March 9 in Aircraft #384. For the crew and the Squadron it was a return to Graz and it was the only no-flak mission they were to fly. The weather was clear over Italy, the Adriatic and Yugoslavia. Tyler had the squadron position pin pointed all the way. But as they approached the southern Alps and Austria the clouds became solid. Without radar equipment it was impossible to get "positive identification" of the target. The secondary target, the steelworks at Kapfenburg, was obscured as well. They returned to base and landed with a full bomb load, a procedure that makes any crew very, very nervous.

The fruitless nature of the trip to Graz initiated another bull session involving two perennial subjects. One subject was the "morality of the bombing war" and the other was related. It was the controversy over the U.S. daylight "pinpoint" bombing vs. the RAF nighttime pattern bombing.

Most of the fliers did not think deeply about the "morality of bombing." They had all <u>volunteered</u> to do a tough job and help end the war. It was an impersonal job. They could see the flak and fighters, but could not see their "victims," if there were any. Most agreed that it was a generous policy not to bomb targets in German occupied countries unless "positively identified." And most agreed that the U.S. strategy would kill a few, but spare many women and children civilians.

All were very disturbed by the stories being circulated about the RAF bombing of Dresden two weeks earlier. The stories claimed that Dresden had been turned into a "fiery furnace"—a huge storm of a fire that engulfed most of the city and the inhabitants and visitors. The 15th had flown many missions to the very gates of Dresden in their relentless pursuit of the Brux oil complex. And they knew that there were no "military" targets in Dresden—regarding it almost as an undeclared "open city." Always the final comment was "we might feel differently if we were Londoners."

The next mission could be called 16 and 1/2. It was flown on the 12th of March. The 353rd was in the high squadron position and the group was going back to Vienna after one more of the smaller refineries. It was a bizarre flight. The weather was good. The group made rendezvous over Vis and headed north climbing all the way to be above the Alps. Rury was the crew officer responsible for oxygen discipline. At 10,000 feet he put the crew "on oxygen." Then, every five minutes he'd go on intercom and say "bombardier to crew—oxygen check." The reply was "tail roger, waist roger, radio roger, ball roger, nose roger, cockpit roger and top turret roger."

From his vantage in the nose Rury was enjoying the marvelous view of the snow covered Alps. A couple of the peaks west of the plane loomed up to 10,000 feet. He initiated an oxygen check. He got only six replies. There was no "top turret roger." Thornton immediately told Narracci to check on Schratz. Narracci swung around and gazed at an apparition—Schratz's face was purple—his oxygen mask was off—his body dangled like a lifeless doll from the butts of the twin 50 caliber turret guns. His left arm had a right angle turn between the elbow and the shoulder. After just one gulp Narracci did the right things. First he put his own oxygen mask over Schratz's mouth. He called for Lake to help him and bring three of the small personal oxygen tanks that were aboard. Together, he and Lake put Schratz's own oxygen mask on him and hooked it to the emergency small tank. Schratz started to show signs of revival. Gingerly they disengaged the mess of the engineer's parachute harness and gun butts that were so entangled. Gently they partially straightened the broken arm and bound the arm to his body using his scarf—and dragged him to the waist where he could be stretched out.

Thornton called the group lead plane and asked permission to return to base. This was granted so they headed south hoping Schratz would be okay. They got no credit for a mission but they saved a life. It also eased their collective conscience about the previous mission.

Schratz later explained that somehow he had accidentally hit the power switch for the turret. Immediately the guns swung around and became entangled in his left sleeve catching the arm and snapping the humerus like it was a tiny twig. His entrapped body was dragged out of his seat, his oxygen mask was knocked off and he couldn't reach his "push to talk" switch to call for aid. Without oxygen he passed out in seconds. Only the discipline of the oxygen check saved his life.

Schratz went to the infirmary and Sgt. Sator Sanchez became the tenth man. The enlisted men called him Sandy and held him in awe. All of squadron should have. Sandy was the only flier in the 301st Bomb Group at that time who had the Silver Star. He received that during his first tour of duty with the Eighth Air Force, flying out of Cambridge, England. He had received the Silver Star because he had helped an injured copilot bring a disabled Fortress back to base with a dead pilot aboard. And, they landed safely because of Sandy's skill and bravery. Sandy had a Purple Heart and *mucho* oak leaf clusters on his Air Medal and a Distinguished Flying Cross. He was the prototype quiet hero. Schratz was a helluva good engineer. It was a tribute to both that Sandy made the team simply by showing up for the next mission.

As the Germans succumbed ever more frequently in military battles with the Fifteenth they raised the level of their psychological warfare to its most shrill. The leading exponent laying siege against the 15th was an American traitor known to the fliers as Axis Sally. Her radio broadcasts could be heard daily. As a "come on" she played records of popular American music. A lot of the content of the messages was propagandish tripe. But she launched warnings aimed against specific components of the 15th. For the first ten days of March she had been repeating for the benefit of the Fifth Wing, the 2000 year old Caesarian warning—"Beware the Ides of March." It was such an insistent and repetitive message that the fliers were beginning to wonder if the Germans had one more surprise in their package. The good weather in March was permitting a mission every day. There were two lead squadrons for the 353rd. Thornton's crew was alternating with another for lead. When they were scheduled for the twelfth they assumed they would fly on the 14th and the 16th—and stay in Lucera on the Ides. But, when they returned early with the wounded Schratz on the 12th they were posted on the BO for the 13th. Now they were flying on the odd days of March.

The mission on the 13th was the seventeenth for the crew and it was one of the most successful. The target was in Germany, which they liked. The target was oil, which they liked. They were going after the last of the huge oil storage tanks in Regensburg. Tyler's navigation was very professional. The weather was good all the way. The rendezvous was on schedule and Tyler hit the IP on his ETA. Rury took over and sighted the Aiming Point in his Norden and twelve 500-pound RDX bombs cascaded downward in unison to hit dead center. The other squadron planes followed suit with exquisite timing. By the time the squadron had rallied from the target Yovich could see huge pillars of smoke billowing upwards. These smoke giants would reach the 20,000 feet level. The inventory of German oil was indeed dwindling. Thornton flew them home aboard #819. Once over the Adriatic the intercom discipline was eased and never had the remarks of the crew been so animated. They could feel the flush of victory.

And the rest of the war news was erupting with excitement. Cologne had fallen to the Yanks. And Patton had breached the Rhine River, capturing intact a bridge at the little known city of Remagen. The Russians were massed at the Oder/Neisse River banks for a future drive on Berlin. The Red Armies were grinding into Germany just as once the Wehrmacht had ground its way toward Moscow in the late months of 1941. The 8th, the 15th and the RAF were flying 3000 bomber sorties a day—pummeling the remaining targets in Deutschland. The Germans had little gasoline and almost less transport capability if they had gasoline to transport. For the Allies the pace of war had risen to a screaming crescendo.

As a squadron lead navigator Tyler became much more familiar with the "inner" world of the Fifteenth Air Force. He became more and more impressed with the emphasis on planning as well as execution. This would stand him in good stead in later years as the first manager of the Dow Corning F.E.C. Business which soon became and remains Dow Corning's largest and most successful Business.

His observations were that the 15th displayed all the elements necessary for a successful action organization. They had an objective: *The unconditional surrender of Germany!* They had a dominant strategy: *Deprive the Nazis of oil.* They had a secondary strategy: *Help the Russians drive back the Germans on the eastern front.*

They had in the top echelons capable people who could develop the near-term—often daily-tactical activities, and support personnel who could plan the details necessary to support the tactics. The tactics were never counter to the strategies. They had adequate resources. They had brave doers—courageous enough to implement the tactical actions. They had both successes and failures in the daily tactics. They took successes in stride and learned from the failures. They never faltered.

On March 14th Thornton was told that his crew had been selected to fly in the group lead spot. Tyler was thrilled for group lead was his ultimate dream as a navigator. Even though a group might fly to the same target as the rest of the Fifth Wing, the group was always an individual entity. The group senior navigator was Captain Lehr. He accompanied Thornton, Narracci and Tyler on a two-hour instructional flight on how the lead plane circles and climbs in order for the entire group to fall into the prescribed formation—a process called the rendezvous. And that was it. Tomorrow they would be one of the two crews that would lead the group. There were always two group lead planes—just in case.

This also meant that they would fly in a plane equipped with Mickey radar navigation equipment. And that meant that the crew would have a new tenth man. The radar equipment was located on the B-17 below the fuselage and behind the bomb rack where normally there is a ball turret. So silent "Scotty," our ball gunner, was transferred to another crew. The new tenth man was Lt. Stephen Stofko. Like Tyler, he was a navigator and hailed also from the hard coal region of eastern Pennsylvania.

For the group, the mission begins when the two lead navigators open the secret orders. Lehr and Tyler were up and in the "ready room" at 3 a.m. They both gasped when they read the summary of the orders. This was no ordinary mission. The target was to be the synthetic oil refinery at Ruhland, Germany, just south of Berlin. It was the number one priority target in all of Europe. It was the only operational oil source remaining to the Germans. The 15th would hit this target in conjunction with the 8th out of England. Only the Fifth Wing of the 15th would fly to Ruhland. This was the only wing of B-17's. All the other heavy bombardment wings were B-24's which did not have the range. This was the longest mission every attempted by any bombers during the five years of war in Europe. The planes would carry full bomb loads (twelve 500-pounders), but would go in at 25,000 feet, a mile lower than usual, in order to stretch the range of the planes. They would pass over the _headquarters_ of Goering's Luftwaffe at Klotsche, near Dresden. Intelligence felt they would encounter the new Jerry jets, the Me-262's.

All of the above was on plan A(ABEL). Lehr and Tyler were excited about the history-making assignment. They drew in the up and back course patterns on the maps . They would rendezvous over Vis and head directly north along the 15th meridian to the IP—no zigging or zagging. From Bautzen to Kamenz to Ruhland. It sounded like a double play combination. Bautzen was the IP and Kamenz was a city halfway down the bomb run. There was no margin for fuel on this extraordinary and lengthy mission. They completed the flight plans and developed an alternate target plan. Thence to briefing to study the reactions of the crews when they heard the mission details.

First off, the weather in Italy was not the best, so Major Paine announced an hour delay in schedule. Tyler headed for the mess hall and polished off a breakfast of pancakes (real butter that day) and went back to his tent, the famed #10. He couldn't tell his three tentmates any details but they could see he was excited and he smiled when he said "I'll get me an FW-190 today."

Then it was back to the briefing. When the target map was displayed there was not a sound, none of the groans when Brux or Blechhammer were due. At first the crews were stunned—and then there was this buzz. After the briefing Thornton's crew, these ten men, went to the plane and climbed aboard #801 with its beautiful radar bubble hanging low from the plane's center. It started to rain and Thornton kept his eye on the tower for the red flare that would "scrub" the mission. But soon it cleared a little and over the radio came the command to "execute Plan Abel!"

The 353rd would be the lead squadron today. The two group lead planes took off first with Thornton off the right wing of the Major's plane. The squadron planes followed and the weather cleared on the way across the Adriatic to Vis. Lehr, the teacher, in the first lead plane screwed up the rendezvous a little but no problem. The 301st, one of the two B-17 groups to fly the first missions out of England two and a half years earlier, was on its history-making way to Ruhland, 700 nautical miles away.

They headed north, climbing a little more slowly than usual. Rury put them on oxygen at 10,000 feet as they passed Venice, Fiume, Trieste and Zagreb. Northward past previous targets of Graz and Wiener-Neustadt and then across the Danube between former targets Linz and Vienna. Higher now, they crossed the frosty white Alps of Austria and into Czechoslovakia, past its capital of Prague, past the once-fearsome target of

Blechhammer, now a rubbled ruin in the Sudetes Mountains, and finally into Germany. They passed Dresden, that once-lovely city which still lay smoldering in its hot ashes from the awesome power of a gigantic fire resulting from an RAF raid a few weeks earlier. Just north of Dresden they could see the air-field at Klotzsche where Goering and his fuelless planes were grounded. None came up to meet them. Maybe Axis Sally's threat to "Beware the Ides of March" had no foundation.

All during this northward flight Stofko was picking up pre-arranged navigational points on his radar. He would relay to Tyler a fix, e.g. "Zagreb twenty miles at bearing 060." Tyler could then recheck the group's ground speed and ETA. It was a super help for the navigator.

Soon Tyler could pick up the IP. They were there exactly at 1350 hours. The IP was Bautzen and Ruhland, the target, lay 29 miles or nine minutes away, a long bomb run. But Intelligence had briefed "there will be no flak except for the last three min-utes from target." Everybody put on flak suits. Tyler wanted one more drift measurement so picked out the town of Kamenz just ahead. At 1353 he adjusted the drift meter for one last check of this important variable—a must for the bombardier to be effec-tive. He was looking through the drift meter when—BLOOM—it hit. Startled, Tyler looked up and saw Rury putting on his chute. Tyler looked for his and could not find it at first. Panic-panic, but there it was sliding back toward the escape hatch. He hooked it with just one buckle and went back to his map. Look-ing out the window he saw the mortal wound the great skycraft had suffered. Like life blood ebbing away, great streams of black oil gushed out and over the cowling. In his mind Tyler could see the blood flowing from the slit throat of a steer that a Rabbi had killed when Tyler was a small boy on the farm.

But he still felt secure in his B-17. Was not this Fortress invul-nerable? And, wouldn't three engines take them wherever they wanted to fly?

After the fatal flak burst Dale Thornton headed the plane north toward the city of Cottbus. He could see the oil pressure on No. 1 plummet. Narracci was already into the feathering pro-cedure—but no response. Dale's first thought was to circle and try to pick up the group on the way south from the target. But they were losing altitude. He ordered Rury to jettison the bombs and Tyler to figure a heading and ETA to the nearest emergency landing field. Tyler gave him an instinctive heading of 095 and started to locate the position of and distance to this landing field. He barked to the crew that they would be over Russian-held territory in five minutes.

The unfeathered prop was beginning to windmill. Narracci was reading the tachometer when it went off the scale at 3000 RPM. You could hear it whine. Lake was watching the engine from the waist. He got on intercom to say "it's *smoking*" and then yelled *"IT'S ON FIRE!"*

That very second Thornton unhesitatingly pulled the bail-out bell. With the bell ringing in his ears Tyler pulled the release of his flak suit, pulled off his earphone and throat mike cords, disconnected the wires leading to his heated flying suit, finally breaking the oxygen line connection. By this time they were at 20,000 feet. Still encumbered by the last grasp of all the tentacles he had just severed, Tyler backed out of the nose to the escape door just rearward from the navigator's desk. He yanked on the red handle and the door flew into the slipstream. He moved to the aft side of the opening and could see Narracci's legs descending toward this escape door. Tyler faced forward and with a short salute to Rury he dove into the nothingness below.

When Tyler was the first to bail out, the ten-man team was parted, never to be united again. Yovich was the second man—exiting at the small emergency door in the tail. Rury should have been third but he hesitated and Narracci saluted him too and dove as the third man. Taylor was the fourth man, followed by Lake, the fifth man. The waist gunners leapt from the burning plane through the main entrance, the door now gone after Taylor pulled the red handle. Rury finally took a deep breath and dove. He was the sixth man. Stofko was lining up behind Lake and behind him was the radio operator, Marich. Stofko went out the main entrance. He was the seventh man. Marich, finding himself fourth in line just before Taylor jumped, decided to go out the open bomb bay doors. He turned and started to go forward to the bomb bay. The delay meant he would not be eighth. Thornton held the burning plane level long enough for the crew to exit. He set the auto pilot and, keeping his eye on the instruments, <u>backed out</u> of the cockpit and descended to the front escape hatch. He got just a glance of Rury's legs disappearing. Then he dove downward too. He was the eighth man. Marich reached the bomb bay aft position and heard a muffled explosion as he dove through this huge exit opening in the dying plane. He was the ninth man.

But what happened to Sandy, the tenth man? No one knows for sure. At the bail-out signal he should have descended from the turret rearward and been the first to exit from the bomb bay opening. The pilots exiting with their eyes forward on the instruments never saw him. By the time Marich went out the bomb bay there was no Sandy to be seen. One theory was that he did not have his chute harness on. Another is that he stayed in his turret and at his guns and rode it down.

The nine who bailed out were captured that very day by the Germans and were POW's until April 29, only 45 days. The site of their capture was a mile west of the town of Bad Muskau in East Germany. Bad Muskau is on the Neisse River, the border now between Poland and Germany and the front line between the Germans and Russians on the Ides of March, 1945.

Forty-five years later Tyler returned to the very spot where the nine men were captured and the plane crashed. He searched and searched for the grave of the tenth man. He was unsuccessful, but plans to return again. Surely the mystery shrouding this incident can be cleared. Where lies the body of this hero?

✪

CHAPTER 3

KRIEGIE

LIFE AS A GERMAN P.O.W.

Shortly after the bail-out bell rang I dove head first into four miles of nothingness. Then it was down—down—down. I kept thinking "delay for 10 seconds—delay, delay and straighten out, straighten out—and down, down, down." The sensation of falling seemed absent and only a simulated wind rushed by. My only sight was my huge flying boots flapping in the breeze and silhouetted against the blue sky and it was down—down—down! By then, (only a few seconds) I started to get dizzy, the first unmistakable sign of anoxia. So I pulled the rip cord with no thought, not even a little prayer, on my mind. Immediately came the sudden jolt and the weakening reaction of realization. That huge white mushroom towering above was temporary refuge enough.

Then, sort of dulled, I started to take stock. Still clutched in a now-bleeding but painless hand was my navigator's pencil. I tucked it away and took off my oxygen mask tossing it down ahead of me.

The earth was still thousands of feet below and my descent was so slow that there was no apparent change in the patterns of the countryside—so no sensation of movement downward. I was just suspended in that awful stillness, gently oscillating and feeling oh so very much alone.

While looking up to stop the oscillating I spied the other chutes. I counted eight others—only one missing. Next I pulled out my .45 and inserted a fresh clip and put one round in the chamber and tucked the gun back into my holster.

Finally the sensation of motion returned as I got nearer the ground. Most of the countryside was a series of small forests and I could tell that I was facing in the correct direction drifting with the wind at my back and headed for the trees. The last hundred feet took only seconds and the evergreens rushed upward like huge green needles ready to ensnare a victim on a point. I doubled up, covered my face and fell on through the branches. My chute caught the high branches and I was very gently deposited on the forest floor.

I had no plan whatsoever. The first action was to unfasten the chute harness and get moving. This I did. After a running step and a half I was snapped back to the chute. I had previously fashioned an escape kit out of a Cracker Jack box and taped it to my chute harness and tied it to my leg. It took ten more seconds to sever the kit from the harness. I was to be forever grateful for some of the items in the escape kit.

Then I ran like a scared rabbit toward the east—either toward the Russians or away from the Germans, depending on which side of the front I had landed. In all those clothes and heavy flying boots it wasn't long before labored breathing demanded a halt. The small forest ended and I crossed a small road and into another patch of trees.

Those forests in Germany weren't the conventional kind, I can tell you. The trees were small and all the underbrush had been removed to show the trees lined up in straight rows. It was next to impossible to hide effectively. I considered this my best plan—hold out until dark and then try to find an old barn in which to hide. If I could find water, I had enough food in my "kit" to hole up for several days.

So I started to crawl down one of the aisles between the trees, keeping as low as I could but knowing I was visible at least 50 yards each way. While on hands and knees I came across a single strand of silvery tinfoil—like an artificial icicle on a Christmas tree. I knew it was a piece of chaff we had discarded from the planes a half hour earlier—to deflect the Germans' Radar sightings. The chaff was like a shaft—a poignant pang in a tender spot—made more tender by the drone of the 301st B-17's heading for Italy leaving behind their five-mile-high vapor trails—and a lonely navigator. I stood up and swallowed hard and for the first time was conscious of the sporadic boom-boom of the guns on the eastern front only a mile away.

So there I lay and waited and hoped and even daydreamed a little as is my wont. But it wasn't long until they came—clattering and clanging through the tiny forest—in extended order with their thick guttural voices making no attempt at stealth. I thought "God bless Brother Timothy for teaching me the rudiments of German." One of the soldiers yelled *"Kom aus—wir sehen"* and I stood up and yelled the faintly comic and Hollywoodish *"Kamerad."* Right then I didn't know but what I might be on my scaffold and I felt that I was. But I could hear *"Hand hochen"* and I yelled back *"Ja, Hand hochen."*

They led me to the German lieutenant. He took my razor blades, toothpaste and soap—but let me keep my razor holder and my tooth brush, and my small cache of food. He retrieved my gun from the young soldier who had it. He made fun of this "inferior" weapon and showed me his Luger—which of course was a beauty. He also got back my heavy flying pants.

He put me under the charge of two young ruffians with Tommy guns and gave some orders to them and off we marched. In the next five minutes I spent the only moments of the war when I was truly terrified. We headed down a narrow road to a deep dark forest. Both the Germans were behind me. My imagination was running riot by then and atrocity stories were foremost. At the edge of the woods I saw one of those ox-drawn vee-shaped manure carts emerge. In my mind's eye I could see it filled with grotesque forms of murdered bodies. In the next seconds I went through the mental anguish of a condemned man heading for the gallows. But there were no shots to ring out and my calm returned. I never hit that low an ebb again.

Then all day long it was walk and talk—walk and talk—new guards and new interrogators. I insisted I flew alone and from Italy. Nobody believed me on either count. I told one lieutenant that I was an arts student and he replied—"yes, the art of destroying our cities." I didn't argue that we almost always went after oil—but there was a grim satisfaction to see not a single motorized vehicle at this sector of the eastern front. There were artillery guns being drawn by oxen and horses. The soldiers had peculiar cigarette lighters—a flint and spark wheel all right, but the spark ignited a several inch long punky rope at the top charred end. When the soldiers lit a cigarette with this lighter they always made a face because of the foul first taste from the punk. When asked why such a stupid lighter the reply was "*nichts benzine.*" Had the strategy of the 15th ever hit home! There were also reminders of the ground battles. Up until now this sector of Germany had been unscathed by the war. But the Russians were massed along the Neisse River a mile away and the Germans knew they would cross the river within a few days. Many of the citizens, therefore, were packing a few belongings on wheelbarrows, baby carriages, or toy wagons and trekking westward. Some were staying put despite the overwhelming fear of the Russians all the Germans felt.

On we walked, generally westward toward Spremberg. My guard spied another soldier on a bicycle and talked him out of this machine. He put me, the prisoner, on the handlebars and started huffing and puffing as he pedaled the two of us down the road. We came next to a small command post. The lieutenant was expecting me. He was partially bald but the remaining hair was jet black, and he kept bellowing his name "oberleutnant Weingarten" over the phone—possibly getting directions for my next move. Two young Germans, looking a little like Hollywood versions of Nazis, could speak English and they started an interrogation. How pissed they were when I would say over and over "*verboten*"—name, rank and serial number only.

The next two guards were old duffers. They were to take me to a certain address, probably just outside of Spremberg. By then it was dark and they marched me up and down this street, looking for "ein und zwanzig." The Wehrmacht was snafued too. They found #21 and another very old MP took over and we headed onward in the dark. He had one of these fluorescent badges around his neck that glowed in the dark. We struggled to converse in German. He was very proud to have served under Rommel in Africa in '41 and '42. He said I reminded him of his own son, who was in the Lutwaffe. At least he knew where he was going and about midnight we arrived at a building which reminded me of the large farmhouse where my Uncle Elmer had lived. He took me up to the second floor and opened the door and inside were Lt. Steve Stofko, the radar navigator, and Sgt. George Marich, the radio operator. We hugged and smiled and exchanged stories. All three were fagged out so it wasn't long before we lay on the floor and went to sleep.

We awoke about nine, I guess, and both Stofko and Marich were surprised and happy to find out that I knew a little German. They said "tell the guards we have to go to the bathroom," which I did. The guards gave us some slices of black bread and some honey. I opened one of the small cans of cheese from my escape kit and we had a tasty breakfast—and then I doled out one square apiece of Hershey's chocolate. At that rate it lasted four days and delicious it was, too. About that time a German civilian came into our room. He seemed very timid and tentative, but could speak a little English. He was the local barber and had heard about these three Americans. At one point he whispered "we know that the war is lost but it is *verboten* to speak of such things." For lunch we had some potatoes and gravy and after lunch two more MPs arrived to be our guards for the next move. But before we marched on they lined us up like we were a prize catch of fish and took our pictures. For the Germans we were celebrities. They were in the grim position to try to hold off the advancing Russians, whom they feared. To capture three American prisoners was an unlikely event. We may be captured forever somewhere in a treasured old German photo album.

On we marched. It was a sunny spring day and in our heavy clothes we were hot. Stofko had only his heavy flying boots for footwear and was having a hard time. Marich had a pair of dress shoes which he had tied to his parachute harness. I was the lucky one. I had heard stories of fliers who had bailed out without proper shoes and suffered for it. So my practice was to wear ankle high walking shoes instead of the electrically-heated slippers that we were supposed to wear. My toes were cold on every mission, but I was prepared to hike now that I was in Germany. Even so my feet were hurting a little too.

The guards stopped at a small village pub. One went in for a beer, and shortly after decided to let the prisoners join the party, so in we went with the other guard. It was my first taste of this good German dark (*schwartze*) beer—and the only beer I would get while a prisoner. I could pick up a little of the conversation. The bartender was saying that the Americans were now bombing tiny villages, citing the damage nearby. Later, when the guards were not near us, I told this story to the others—since the damage to the village was from the very bombs which Rury had jettisoned the day before.

We marched until midnight and must have been in or near Spremberg. The guards took us to a filthy old jail and put us all in a single cell. Without really thinking about the situation I said in German to the jailer "only two beds?" He growled back "*ja, nur zwei Bette*." We could see that we must remember that the Germans did not like us very much.

A short while later the cell was opened and in came this huge Russian prisoner. He was a captain in the Russian Air Force and he was terrifically burned on his hands, face, arms and legs. His burns were loosely wrapped with torn shreds from his own parachute. He was the pilot of a Bell Aircobra P-39 and claimed that he had 45 victories to his credit—truly one of the outstanding aces of the war.

He could speak a little English but was quite good in German. So here we were, two soldiers made friends by our trips into the "wild blue yonder," conversing in the language of the enemy. While we were prisoners of the Germans, we knew then that we were the victors. The Russian ace was vehement in his forecast that the war would be over in "*ein monat*."

Marich and Stofko dozed off in the "*nur zwei Bette*." Captain Kaparov and I continued talking—mostly in my halting German. He confided in me a well-kept secret of the war, an astounding story. He said that he had been to Alaska several times over the "*geheimer Luftrasse*"(secret air route). He claimed that for over two years dozens of USSR fliers had been picking up U.S. warplanes—mostly fighter planes. The German word is *jagdflugzeuge*, "hunter" airplane, but also numerous "*bombenflugzeuge*," over ten thousand airplanes in total. The fighter planes were P-39's and P-63 King Cobras all made by Bell. Most of the bombers were A-20's but a thousand were B-25's.

The captain was one of the first in this ferry command, a group who called themselves "*der erste Ritter der verdienst Legion*," the first knights of the Legion of Merit. He and his comrades had received the American Legion of Merit, authorized by FDR himself. American fliers flew the planes to Fairbanks. The Russians picked them up and flew (in about ten hops) across the Bering Straits, Siberia and eventually to Moscow. They would return on this "*geheimer Luftrasse*" in C-47's for a repeat journey. Kaparov always flew P-39's. He loved that Air Cobra for it was ideal to take on the Luftwaffe and to support the ground troops, which Kaparov had been doing for over a year.

In effect, the mighty U.S. industrial effort during the war had sent to Europe first the Eighth Air Force and then the Fifteenth Air Force and, in addition, had equipped this "geheimer Air Force"—a potent factor in the amazing Russian victory over the Germans.

On the day we buried Grandpa Tyler, June 22, 1941, Hitler launched Operation Barbarossa (Red Beard), the affectionate name of King Frederick I of Germany. What Hitler had overlooked was that Barbarossa, while leading a Crusade, had died ignominiously by drowning while trying to cross a river. Now Hitler was drowning—in the blood of millions of Germans. Hitler disdained the Russians, calling them *untermenschen* (subhuman). How wrong! This Russian ace, this mighty warrior who whispered this amazing story to me was the epitome of valor, intelligence, and pride. How fortunate we were to have such staunch allies, whom we could help in removing the scourge of fascism. Kaparov, truly, was Thor's Hammer.

After the story this giant soldier slumped some more and said so hoarsely now "*Schmerzhaft*" (painful). I called the jailer and told him the Captain needed medical aid for his burns. He finally agreed and led the Captain out of the jail. I was to see him once more. In the late morning we three Americans were being moved . About a quarter mile from the jail we saw two men come out of a building. One was German, the other was a Frankenstein—a giant whose hands, arms and legs and head were swaddled in clean bandages. I saluted this hero and we parted ways.

Shortly after our last glimpse of the Russian ace we heard what was a familiar sound to all Germans—the high pitched and high decibel sound of an air raid siren. The guards took us down into the cellar of a factory. All the Jerry civilians there looked daggers at us each time the bombs hit. The target was Ruhland again, taking another pasting.

On we hiked. Again we noticed the complete absence of gasoline powered vehicles. Almost all of the buildings were deserted—the factories were closed and a few people were packing up a small collection of belongings to join the procession of people trekking westward and trundling a few possessions in small wagons. Defeat was in the air everywhere.

The guards took us to an airport. I overheard part of the conversation in German. We were not supposed to be brought there. For us, though, it was an interesting chance to see some of the Jerry planes from up close. One of the planes looked just like a Piper Cub, the only plane I knew how to fly. In my mind's eye I daydreamed of running over to the tiny plane, spinning the prop, climbing in and racing (60 knots) the few miles to Russian territory. But the reality was that it started to rain, and on we went, getting soaked to the skin. The smell of wet simulated fur on my flying jacket waved over me—an odor I would live with many more times. We finally arrived at our destination. It was a guard house near a coal mine at the edge of a small city named Senftenberg (Mustard City).

This entire area we were in was on the fringes of Silesia. Vast deposits of brown coal had been mined in this section of Europe for centuries. The coal was the raw material that was converted to oil by reaction with hydrogen gas. So coal mining had the same priority as the much-needed oil. At the Senftenberg mine German soldiers were doing double duty. They wore uniforms on one shift, then they donned miner's clothes and put in a shift down in the coal mine. These double-duty Germans were our guards for two days. The evening we arrived we were wet and cold and tired so could fall asleep on the floor immediately.

We stayed inside the guard house all the next day. We had a chance to wash—without any soap—a luxury that most Germans had not seen for over a year. I understood now why the lieutenant at the front had taken my soap. So we were beginning to feel grimy—and bearded, since I had also lost the blades for my razor to the same lieutenant. The guard shift kept changing. There was one soldier, a large Nordic Nazi, who kept up a constant harangue once he knew I could understand a little German. It was unbelievable that he was convinced that Germany would win the war. He kept repeating this, as if the verbal description of the act often enough would make it true. He had this little black book full of "facts." He ranted about "*die Jude.*" His little book listed how many Jews lived in London and in New York City and in Miami. He decried their alleged worldwide plot to seize the reins of power through money. He kept looking at Stofko, who was a husky, handsome, blonde young man. He asserted that Steve must, in reality, be a German. He invited all three of us to "take the pledge." Like most Germans he denigrated the Russians. Despite his bombast, boasting, and irrational view of the war, the Russians would take this coal mine—and maybe him—two weeks later.

Twenty-four hours after we got there they gave us a meal. We were hungry but simply could not finish those greasy potatoes. We slept on the floor again.

On the 19th of March we left Senftenberg with two guards, one a Czech, who could speak English. We hiked for a while but eventually got to a railroad station and boarded a train. On the train I sat next to the Czech. Forty-five years later I can remember two parts of his conversation. One I knew without his telling me—that I did not speak German very well. The other was his interest in whatever had happened to Shirley Temple. I told him that Shirley was now a young teenager and had not made a movie in several years. We rode this train for several hours—moving very slowly—and eventually arrived at a spot that I had marked well on my group lead navigator's chart for the Ruhland mission. It was the headquarters for the Luftwaffe—and Herman Goering himself—at Klotzsche, a suburb of Dresden, about six miles north of the city.

The jailer there was a gruff, old, loud son of a bitch. He took my watch, my ring (University of Scranton), a navigator's wings bracelet, what food I had left, then put me into solitary. As he took each item from me he had a young teenage girl make a record. She wrote in that old fashioned, flowery script—*einen Ringen silber* etc.,—as if making the record made the stealing legal.

I spent the entire day of the 20th in solitary. The cell was long and high and narrow. There was a tiny window about 15 feet from the floor. The cell door had a small window also. The teenage girl who recorded the thefts kept looking in the window periodically, smiling always and teasing I suspect. I had one meal that day—some not very good cabbage and dark bread. There was aught to do but pace the cell, peer out the small window in the door and pace some more. Darkness fell and the cell grew colder. There was no blanket, no furniture except a wide wooden shelf about bed-high with an inclined plane of wood to serve as a pillow. My heavy flying jacket and pants were my allies that night.

The next morning the old jailer and another guard took the three of us and we headed onward only dimly aware of the unforgettable impact that day would bring. From Klotzsche we traveled southward toward the heart of Dresden on a streetcar or trolley—an almost exact replica of the Scranton trolleys I rode so many times. The closer we got to the center of the city the more horrific the bomb damage. In Italy I had heard stories of the huge fire that resulted from RAF raids on Dresden a few weeks earlier. The center of the city was completely demolished and smoldered still. Thousands upon thousands of civilians had died in the storm of fires from the terrible raids. The shriveled corpses had been excavated from the cellar shelters where the people died. They were piled into huge heaps amidst the ruins of the city and their partial cremation was then completed. The stench of burnt flesh hung like a pall over the city.

As the trolley entered this realm of death and destruction in center Dresden the bastardly old jailer started to incite the passengers on the streetcar with his harangue about the evil Allied bomber crews. He ranted about *"Amikanischer Kultur"*—that our targets were "*keine Fabriken, nichts Industrie*" but "*die Fraue und Kinder.*" A crowd started to gather around the trolley making more and more threatening gestures and screaming obscenities We three felt that a lynching was almost in progress—and we were to be the lynchees. At that point the high notes of an air raid siren cleared the streets of people. Everybody left the trolley and the guards decided to keep us moving. We hiked through the deserted city with the intermittent wail of the sirens interrupting the stillness. We walked through the streets, little more than paths cleared by shoving the rubble of destroyed buildings aside. The only structures still standing were the few tall circular brick smokestacks—their circular geometry and heat-resistant design making them impervious to both blast and fire.

We arrived at a point where an intact bridge extended across the Elbe River. There was a tall hill and an old University campus on the north shore of the river. We were on the city outskirts and away from the area of extreme bomb damage. I was so distressed by what I had seen that I wept inwardly at what we humans were doing to these humans. And it was so against the norms and directives of the Fifteenth Air Force. All of our targets had been oil refineries, oil storage depots, or railroad marshalling yards. General Eaker, the leader of the Mediterranean Air Forces, was an outspoken proponent of the strategic air war we had been fighting. In fact, on January 1 he had protested publicly against "terror bombing" and insisted that the MAAF would not have the least part in such tactics. Eaker had written to General Spaatz, the Supreme U.S. Air Commander in Europe, advising him "against sending heavy bombers to attack transportation targets in small German towns, for there would be many civilian casualties and the German people might be convinced that the Americans were barbarians, just as National Socialist propaganda charged." He added "We should never allow the history of this war to convict us of throwing the strategic bomber at the man in the street."

But now I could see firsthand that this once-beautiful city was the victim of terror bombing and knew that we three faced a justifiably wrathful populace. More than twice as many people were killed in the Dresden raid than were killed in Hiroshima. We faced the people's wrath at the site of the Elbe Bridge and the old university. The sirens ended their wail and people and traffic were stirring again. It was obvious that the guards were going to wait at this spot to "hitchhike" a ride in our movement. Some civilians would stop and gape at us. I was labeled a "*Schweinhund*" over and over. One old lady clenched her fist and shouted at us in English "Murder Corporation." I had this urge to correct her and say it was "Murder Incorporated." Murder Incorporated was the press caption for a mob of professional hit men operating in Brooklyn before the war. In a demonstration of extremely poor taste one of the Eighth Air Force B-17's had been given the name of "Murder Incorporated" and this bomber with its offensive name on the nose had been captured by the Germans. Goebbles, the propaganda master, seized on this incident to add to the stories about the barbarian American fliers.

We were greatly relieved when a truck stopped and the guards and we climbed aboard and crossed the Elbe, leaving the ghostly, charred and almost dead city of Dresden behind. My attitude toward a bombing war was changed forever. The truck we boarded burned <u>charcoal</u>. I had yet to travel a mile on a <u>gasoline</u> powered vehicle. We rolled westward on this smoky behemoth and later that day arrived at another very large city, Leipzig. Central Leipzig was demolished too, but the stench of death was not there. No smoldering fires burned and no piles of human ash marked mass graves as in Dresden. In center city the sirens whined their song again. This time the guards took us to an air raid shelter. Down in the shelter I could feel the weight of the hate the civilians directed at us poor three still attired in our allied flying garb with the little American flag on the right shoulder of our jackets (the flags were to protect us in case we were captured by the Russians instead of the Germans).

At "all clear" we exited the shelter and walked from there to the railroad station—or what had been the railroad station. Once it had been a grand structure. It was huge—built like a gigantic Quonset hut with its spacious oval windowed roof. The magnificent archway was now a shell. Not a single pane of glass remained. Through the open spaces there lay in all directions piles of rubble and not a building intact or even recognizable. Still the trains ran—coal-burning steam-driven trains. We boarded one and headed southwest along the Saale River eventually arriving at our next stop, the city of Weimar. Weimar had suffered very little bomb damage so was more representative of pre-war Germany. That was fitting, for it was there that the Third Republic was born. In the grim days of 1918 after Germany surrendered the country almost went Communist and might have become another of the socialist Republics of USSR. Here in Weimar the new president vowed to fight Bolshevism and thus won the support of the military, an alliance that kept the Weimar Republic alive until the evil of the Nazi took over. Weimar is also noted as the city of the great German poet, Goethe, who is buried there. We stopped for just awhile at the Gestapo headquarters in Weimar. They had no interest in us and the guards were instructed to move us to the nearby Dulag Luft. Not so nearby it turned out. That was because we walked all of the way. The old guard had picked up a very attractive fraulein as a companion. She walked too. About 2 a.m. we arrived at the Dulag and into solitary we went.

The next morning I moved out of the solitary cell for some preliminary interrogation. Interrogation of captured Allied airmen was the sole purpose of the Dulag Luft organization and they went at it with zest and competence. While outside the cell I got a glimpse of our waist gunner, Lake, and our tail gunner, Yovich. I had a chance to talk briefly with Yovich, who told me that Thornton, Narracci, Rury and Taylor had left the Dulag just yesterday. That meant that nine of the ten crew members were alive and well. Only Sanchez was still unaccounted-for.

Then it was back to solitary—part of the interrogation process—isolation and no food or water. The next morning it was my turn for the full treatment. It was fascinating. I was ushered into this magnificent office room with a handsome German captain behind the ornate desk. His spoken English was letter perfect—but with an odd accent. He had lived in Australia for many years as a youth.

To make me feel at ease Captain Hammer first offered me a Lucky Strike and then a glass of Cutty Sark. I declined both. He looked a little quizzical. What he didn't realize was that I had never smoked a cigarette or had a glass of whisky. I did not decline the Milky Way that he next proffered. His technique was obtuse. For fifteen minutes he impressed me with what he knew. He started by opening a huge book—about 6 inches thick. This book contained data about all the American Air Force Bomb Groups. He leafed to the 301st—and the 353rd Squadron. He told me the exact date when I had arrived there and that Maj. Paine had just been promoted (only the week before). He told me I had graduated from the University of Scranton and had completed navigator's training on March 4, 1944 in Hondo, Texas. He said that he was a pilot. He showed me a picture of himself by a B-17, one that the Germans captured intact. He said he had flown it many times and that it was a good plane. Then he got to the point. He asked when I had taken my training in radar navigation. Now I knew he was fishing. In point of fact, I knew nothing about our radar navigational equipment. I think he sensed that. In any case, he was always the gentleman and eventually—after offering me another cigarette—the interview was over. Later Stofko told me that Captain Hammer quizzed him at great length about the radar. He showed Stofko close up photos of captured Mickey equipment and alleged that he had flown in a captured plane and had used this equipment himself. What a smooth operator!

Later that day the five members of our crew were all put in the same cell. It was a good reunion and we each related special aspects of the last week. Yovich had been told by the Germans who captured him that Sgt. Sanchez was dead. It was then that I first heard the weird story that Sanchez never wore a parachute harness—as if by defying fate as he had so many, many times he would retain his invulnerability. Lake said that Sandy was thrilled by the Ruhland assignment. As they boarded our ill-fated 17 Sandy told him "Today we will see the real action." He was the only one who did not survive.

In the evening we were served our first really good meal in a week. It was simple fare—hot soup and black bread. But it was good fare and there was lots of it. We were told that we would be moving on about midnight. There was a lot of train and truck travel at night in Germany in those waning days of the war. The darkness removed the constant threat of low flying fighter planes that harassed the trains in particular.

At 1 a.m. on March 24 there were eighteen captured Americans who left the Dulag Luft on the way to a prison camp. We were getting used to being referred to as *Kriegsgefanganen* (prisoners of war). The Germans who spoke English would always say "for you the war is over." Not by a long shot! We first boarded another charcoal-burning truck which took us to a railroad. We were all placed in a single boxcar and rode that for several hours. At a major rail center we were transferred to a passenger train. The train was jammed and everybody stood. We rode that train for hours, stopping frequently and seeming to back up and then go forward some more. In general we were heading south all that day. I was getting hungry when it occurred to me that I might be able to barter something for some food. I noticed a young soldier eyeing my beautiful gloves. These were long gauntlet gloves of exquisite leather. They were lined with an electrical circuit for external heating in the -50 degree airplane temperature environment. The young soldier said "*schone Handschuhe*." I asked in German if he had anything to eat. He reached in his pack and withdrew a large piece of Thuringer sausage. So, when the guards were not looking our way we made the trade. I stashed the sausage in my jacket and would break off a piece now and then and eat it or give it to Stofko or one of the other crew members. Man, did we ever get thirsty!

Late at night we arrived at the train station in Nuremberg. From there the eighteen of us, with a few guards, started to walk south from center city under the ghastly light of the full moon. Ghastly was the word because Nuremberg was no more. This was the third large city I had seen—all gutted and torn and leveled and gone. It was so quiet. We saw no citizens on our march. The streets were lanes lined with 15-feet-high piles of rubble. The eerie light exposed the dead city more so than the full light of day. After an hour or so we passed a sight that I had seen in the Movietone News. Nuremberg was the birthplace of the Nazis.

Hitler had constructed there a huge stadium for his Nazi rallies. The massive seating area was built of concrete in terraced layers. These seats were relatively free of bomb damage. The extensive concrete parade ground between the bleachers was pockmarked but still grand in its scope. The huge pillared background that soared skyward at the end of the stadium was almost completely destroyed by the bombs. How fitting that we eighteen captured airmen would hold the last rally in Nuremberg Stadium. I told the others where we were and the irony of it all. We stood erect and marched as victors—not as the captured vanquished.

Well after midnight we arrived at the prison camp area. The building outside the main camp was used for processing incoming prisoners. It was so late that all that was done was to give us a meal, some cigarettes and put us in a large cell with quite a few triple tiered bunks. As exhausted as we were we all fell asleep in moments. The next morning we were processed—our names recorded in the book along with the new number, the *Kriegsgefangenen* number, and were issued a metal tag with our number inscribed—one more dogtag to wear.

At 9 a.m. we marched through the gates of the prison camp. This was Stalag Luft #3 in Langwasser, a suburb of south Nuremberg. We were assigned to Barracks #34 of Compound 2. Narracci, Rury and Thornton were already in Compound 2, so there was a brief reunion. At first the older prisoners were interested in us, hoping that we might have news of the war or of their combat units. After that brief moment we became just some more "*Kriegies*," the short version of *Kriegsgefanganen*, the German word for POWs.

We learned first that there were two meals a day—one was of German food at late morning and the second from food that arrived in Red Cross parcels periodically. The first meal was a revelation. It consisted of a bowl of soup—referred to as the "green death"—and a chunk of sawdust-extended black flour bread. There were no eating utensils. There were a lot of maggots floating on my soup. I delicately picked them out with thumb and finger and discarded them. The older Kriegies smiled as they gulped the soup, maggots and all. After that first meal I decided I needed a spoon. I acquired the oval top to a cocoa can and found a length of reasonably stiff steel wire. From the wire I fashioned a handle and with a couple of stones pounded the oval tin lid into a concave shape and bent the edges around the wire handle—not elegant but functional.

The second meal of the day was equally sparse, but better. We received a chunk of Spam and a large slice of cheese and some more black bread. That second Red Cross meal a day was what kept us *Kriegies* alive.

When Stofko and I were assigned to Barracks #4 we found out that there was just one empty bunk. For most of the week we slept two to the bunk until another empty became available. One of the most fascinating aspects of barracks life was the presence of a large number of British fliers. Many were from the RAF of course, but there were prisoners who flew with the Royal Canadian, the Royal Australian and the Royal South African Air Forces as well. British young men were far more articulate than Americans—and they always had lots to say. In subsequent years I would visit Great Britain many, many times, but this was my introduction to the nuances of the separate countries—for we had Scotch and Welsh as well as English RAF flying officers. I was pleased to learn that in the RAF it was not uncommon for the navigator to be the senior officer <u>and the airplane commander.</u>

The British airmen, in particular, loved to talk to the new "*Kriegies*" about their earlier experiences as POWs. Some of them had been prisoners for almost five years. Those who were captured before 1945 had spent time in the original Stalag Luft 3 located in Sagan, Germany, a small town in Silesia just a few miles east of where I had been captured on March 15. Sagan is now a part of Poland since after the war a sizeable sector of Germany was ceded to the Poles.

The old timers almost relished recounting their grim odyssey in vacating Sagan just two months earlier. In the first days of January, it became apparent that the Russians would arrive at Sagan before long. Naturally the Germans would not permit the repatriation of about 10,000 highly skilled Allied airmen. So the prisoners were sure they would probably have to move westward to a new location—and probably by walking. They were all ordered to begin walking the perimeter of the compound every day, to put in at least five miles and get their bodies used to marching. This was good advice. They did exercise but they also realized that most had no decent footwear and nothing like a haversack or pack. They began to improvise.

By mid-January they could hear the sounds of battle daily as the Russians continued their inexorable drive westward. On January 27 they were very close. At 8:30 p.m. the Germans gave the order "Be ready to march within the hour." Four hours actually elapsed before the westward trek began. And, just after midnight the wind began to blow and the snow began to fall. All through the darkness the ill-clad Kriegies with shirt packs or blanket rolls or just cardboard box packs marched and the temperature dropped steadily. On they went facing the relentless wind-driven snow—first to Halbau and then to Freiwaldau. They were so exhausted that the men would sprawl in the snow during the occasional ten minute rest stops. At Freiwaldau—18 miles from Sagan—there were some vacated concentration camp buildings that provided shelter for awhile. They continued marching in the snow until they reached Bad Muskau (where I was captured). Here they were allowed to rest inside— the church, the school, the factory buildings, etc. By February 2 they reached Spremberg, where about half of the 10,000 were herded into the fabled 40 and 8 boxcars for a train trip to Nuremberg. The other half were sent to *Stammlager* VII-A in Moosburg.

At Nuremberg there was a prison camp, XIII-D, which had housed Italian prisoners, who were being relocated as able-bodied workers for the Reich. The Luftwaffe took over XIII-D and it now became what Sagan had been, Stalag Luft 3. At Sagan boredom was a common complaint. In the two months in Nuremberg the *Kriegies* were seldom bored—primarily because of the numerous air raids—especially the nighttime RAF raids where the bombs were dropped promiscuously.

Another fascinating story about POW life at Sagan was told by the older old timers. There were five compounds in the camp there. Most of the American officers were in the central and west compounds. The British officers were in the north compound. In all of the compounds there was a lot of activity centered on escape attempts. But it was in the British compound that the inmates conceived and executed the most elaborate plan. This execution took almost the entire year of 1944. The effort was organized by departments—forgery, map making, compass making, tailoring of civilian clothes, and most of all tunneling.

The plan was simple in concept, but audacious to contemplate The 1,200 Kriegies in the north compound would dig a long tunnel with the exit port inside the forest which bordered the north compound. All 1,200 prisoners would escape through the tunnel on the same night, once the tunnel was completed. The boldness of the plan was continually emphasized to the participants because the German guards and "ferrets" made inspections several times daily. The details of this yearlong endeavor are described in Paul Brickhill's excellent book "The Great Escape." And, in uncharacteristic Hollywood fashion, this book was translated in faithful detail into the fine movie of the same name.

All of the prisoners in Barracks 34 were officers, so were not required to do any labor for the captors. All we had was an ample supply of free time. There was an early morning "*Appel*," or roll call. This required only a counting of the Kriegies by the German guards, whom we called "goons." Once the correct number was verified we were free to follow our own schedule for the next 24 hours. The only obligatory aspects of the schedule were the two meals. As mentioned the second meal was based on food received in Red Cross parcels. All of these were given to the communal mess officer, who was scrupulous in passing out equal portions at mealtimes to each Kriegie. The nonfood items in the Red Cross packages were cigarettes, which were also divided evenly. I saved all of my cigarettes for bartering purposes. They were to become very valuable in a few more weeks.

At one end of the compound there was a bulletin board. Each day the Germans posted a one or two-page "newspaper" mostly containing news about the war. The Germans did not falsify the war news itself. But they persisted in reporting what happened two or three weeks ago as if it had happened yester-day. When I first got there the first reports of Patton's crossing of the Rhine were just being reported, for example. But we did get a true report on the news each day. Somewhere hidden in the compound was a radio, its location known by very, very few of the *Kriegies.* No matter! Somebody tuned into BBC frequently and made a copy of the most pertinent of the war news. Each evening we would gather at the barracks, the two doors would be closed and guards posted in case any "goons" were to arrive unexpectedly. When the okay was given a "reporter" would give us a news report. Always the reporter was British, often Welsh, with that marvelous well-modulated voice confirming the illusion we were actually listening to BBC.

The news of most interest, of course, was the specific progress of the Third Army. Patton's army was making progress eastward at a very steady pace, advancing 10, and sometimes 20 miles a day. It was easy to tell this pace would bring the Ameri-can troops to Nuremberg in about ten days.

The old timers were insistent in reminding us what had happened in Sagan when the Russians were only ten days away a few months earlier. Since walking was the most common form of exercise readily available almost all of us walked a few miles each day. I started walking even more as the pros-pects of a forced march loomed ahead . I soon became a little lame because with each step my right shoe would flex in such a way as to create a sore spot on the Achilles' tendon. I decided I needed a knife to cut away the offending portion of my right shoe. At one end of my barracks there was a broken window. When no guards were near I removed one half of the window frame. From one corner of the frame I removed the right angle corner brace. After straightening it out I had a piece of metal about five inches long. For about two days I kept hammering one edge of this piece of metal between two stones. Eventually the metal strip assumed a very narrow triangle-shaped cross section. The other consequence of this pounding was a scimi-tar shape to the sharp edge of the blade. I whittled a handle for the blade and attached it with some fine wire someone gave me. After whetting the blade's edge I was pleased when the knife was sharp enough to cut a leather flap above the heel of my right shoe. And my sore tendon healed! The true test of the knife was the way it survived the many times I used it to slice the hard sour dark bread that was part of the ration from the Germans.

Everybody in the compound had plenty of cigarettes, but nobody had matches. Whenever a smoker wanted to "light-up" he sought out the nearest buddy who had a lit cigarette. I never did solve the minor mystery of "who lit the first cigarette early each morning?" While there were lots of cigarettes there was only <u>one</u> deck of cards. It was the most ancient, spots -shuffled-off greasiest deck ever seen. The cards were limp from all the bending and the deck was twice the thickness as when new. Four bridge players, who owned the cards, had been playing together for over a year and could almost read each others' minds. On they played hour after hour. I watched over their shoulders often, intrigued by what seemed like a mysterious and complicated game. I vowed to learn one day.

Shortly after we arrived at Stalag #3 the first news about our crew's last mission was reaching home. One day less than two weeks from the Ides of March telegrams were sent to the next of kin of each of the ten crew members on our fateful sortie.

PA 359 42 GOVT=WUX WASHINGTON DC 28 200P
MRS FREDA H TYLER=
981 RICHTER ST SCRN=

THE SECRETARY OF WAR DESIRES ME TO EXPRESS HIS DEEP REGRET THAT YOUR SON 1LT LESLIE J TYLER HAS BEEN MISSING IN ACTION OVER GERMANY SINCE FIFTEEN MARCH 45 IF FURTHER DETAILS OR OTHER INFORMATION ARE RECEIVED YOU WILL BE PROMPTLY NOTIFIED=
ULIO THE ADJUTANT GENERAL.
1/LT 45.

There was more news in an accompanying letter. It was a personal letter from none other than General Twining himself, commander of The Fifteenth Air Force.

Mrs. Freda H. Tyler
981 Richter St.
Scranton, Pennsylvania

My dear Mrs. Tyler:

I deeply regret that I must confirm the notification which you have received from the War Department concerning your son, First Lieutenant Leslie J. Tyler, 0-874093, who has been missing in action since March 15, 1945. Undoubtedly, your concern for his safety has been great. As I am unable to give you any assurance as to his fate, perhaps the few facts we have relative to his recent mission will be of interest to you.

On the above date, Leslie was serving as navigator aboard a Flying Fortress, which was on a bombing mission over the Ruhland synthetic oil plant in Germany. Returning airmen state that shortly after the formation had entered the target area, the bomber received a flak hit which disabled the craft. The stricken ship left the formation almost immediately and began to lose altitude. When last seen, the plane was flying under control below the flight. Since that time no word has been received concerning the fate of the crew. Should there be any change in your son's status, you may be sure that the War Department will notify you immediately.

The designated beneficiary will receive Leslie's personal possessions in due time, through the Effects Quartermaster, Army Effects Bureau, Kansas City, Missouri.

Much of the credit for the many successes we have had during the past months is due to the courage and ability of men like your son. For the part he has played in this battle against the aggressor, Leslie has been awarded the Air Medal with one Oak Leaf Cluster. It is my earnest hope that before very long, we shall hear some word of his safety.

Very sincerely yours,

N. F. TWINING
Major General, USA
Commanding

The warm and positive tone of the general's letter somewhat assuaged the shock of the cold telegram. My brother was working for Western Union at that time and he knew full well the impact of the "yellow envelope syndrome." The news about the ten new MIAs spread quickly as each local newspaper added a short story and photograph. It was a daily occurrence in those days.

Meanwhile, back in Number 3. March 29 marked the end of my second week of captivity—a short period but as jam-packed as any period in my life. On that day an event occurred that in itself was uneventful, but it was another signal about the collapsing German Command and Control. A handful of infantry POWs were brought in to our Stalag Luft. The Luftwaffe commanded all the Stalag Lufts and had been meticulous in incarcerating there only airmen prisoners up to now. A few of the infantry prisoners wore the red keystone patch of the 28th Division whose nucleus was the Pennsylvania National Guard. They were captured in the German counterattack in December. Neither of them knew my good buddy from Dunmore High School, Ted Hart, who had been slugging it out on the front line since the 28th had moved into Normandy months before.

The infantry boys told a bizarre story. They were interred in a German Stammlager for infantry Kriegies near Hammelsburg. One of the prisoners there was General Patton's son-in-law. About two days earlier a small group of soldiers from the 14th Armored Division were organized in to a unit called "Task Force Baum" led by Captain Baum. Ten tanks and crews penetrated the German defenses on the "front" very easily and raced 20 miles to Hammelsburg. There they picked up Patton's son-in-law and quite a few other prisoners and prepared to race back to their unit. In the meantime the Germans figured out what was going on and encircled the task force. The encirclement was so complete that no battle ensued. So the prisoners were free for only an hour or so. They were recaptured along with the "Task Force Baum." Later, after the war, Patton denied vehemently that he had personally ordered "Task Force Baum" on its fateful failed mission.

Another Infantry prisoner came to our camp the next day. He was Colonel Good. Good was a West Point graduate and the ranking colonel in the entire US Army. He was a good old boy, but he soon let us know that he was "in charge." Soon we were keeping a tight formation at Appel. All the measly, weird beards were shaved, but some of the beautiful mustaches were allowed. Good got us to exercise more regularly. He bargained hard with the Germans to get us some medicines and other medical supplies. He organized a "medic" group and got us to pay stricter attention to personal hygiene and to stop spitting where and when we chose. I had graduated pre med from the University of Scranton so could appreciate more his concerns about the threat of Typhus or such similar plagues that could lay us low. He gave us all instructions to make whatever meager preparations we could for marching, emphasizing that the Germans would give us very short notice when, not if, we would move.

The last day of March was uneventful but the night was exciting. The RAF was out in force that night. They were bombing close to Nuremberg, but I knew from my full moon march a week earlier that there was no target worth a 500-pound bomb anywhere near our Stalag. But at night and with the "carpet" bombing pattern employed we had a right to be nervous. After one fairly close resounding boom even the RAF fliers joined in a chorus of the Air Corps "Off we go into the wild blue yonder, flying high into the sun." The next day was Easter Sunday and what a surprise. In the morning after Appel a *bona fide* chaplain came into camp for an hour. He was captured, along with a few other infantry soldiers, in the "Battle of the Bulge." He was Episcopalian but quite a few other Protestants and Catholics gathered around as he soothed our souls with his simple message of redemption (freedom). Then on he went to yet another prison camp later that Easter Day.

In the next few days the weather improved, the meals got smaller, and the talk of our impending "march" took over the conversation. In our combat squadron in Italy the number one, two, three and four topics day after day had been American women, former girl friends, Italian women, and sexual fantasies. In the Stalag the major topic of conversation was *food*—usually food we envisioned we would have in the future, but often on how to modify our sparse food ration to make it more palatable. There were recipes for cakes and pancakes that were quite good. But often small portions of food of any sort were mixed at random for the sake of variety. Our rule was that if it is edible going in it will be edible in any random mixture possible. The one food that Kriegies had available most often was Klim (spell it backwards). Klim was powdered milk, and not bad. It came in the Red Cross parcels and was packaged in cans similar to a coffee can. The Klim can was the standard unit of volume measure for all Kriegies.

With all this talk of food I started to focus on a dish which was popular in the Depression years because it was zero cost. Each year, before the dandelion yellow flowers bloomed, my mother would have me go out and dig the dandelion greens with my knife. You know the knife, encased in a little buttondown leather pouch on the outer side of my right high top boot. A pair of boots like that was ecstasy for an eighth grader. In any case, here in the prison camp I could see a lot of dandelion greens. Around the compound there was a barbed wire fence—only two strands. Then there was a second fence, very high and tough about 20 yards from the first fence. The Nazi guards could shoot any Kriegie who ventured into the annular space between these two fences. It was in this space that the dandelions grew. By keeping an eye on the guards I could quickly reach through the inner fence and dig a dandelion green. After I had about a dozen plants I borrowed a small tin can stove and, using a Klim can as a pot, I cooked my "dandelion greens." But I had no salt and no vinegar. The Klim cooked greens were not like mother used to make.

On Easter Monday evening the secret daily news broadcast was exciting. BBC reported that Patton's Army had advanced 75 miles in a single day and were at the <u>outskirts of Nuremberg.</u> We knew they were close because the artillery sounds were getting very loud. Of course, thoughts of liberation the next day were in the mind of each of us. On April 3 there was no signal to move. But the artillery sounds were closer. Colonel Good assigned Major Hines to be in charge of Barracks 4. For the impending march

Hines would be in charge of several sections. Our section leader would be Captain Carlson, a downed P-51 pilot. Carlson suggested that we form small teams of three each—because the Red Cross parcels would be issued one parcel per three Kriegies. Stofko and I had become acquainted with a former P-47 (Thunderbolt) pilot named Leon Tracy. We called him "Dick Tracy" and he became the third member of our marching team. The BBC broadcast that night confirmed that the Third Army was at the gates of Nuremberg. We were sure we would start the march tomorrow.

CHAPTER 4

✪

FRIENDLY FIRE

Bill Logan was a bombardier. Bill Logan was married, a father, a Kriegie and an excellent athlete. Bill Logan was a good Catholic. He died in a "State of Grace."

As I remember it, Bill grew up in Brooklyn. His father's name was Michael and he ensured that Bill would have a fine education. Bill attended St. Brendan's school and then St. John's Preparatory School. He earned his bachelor of science degree from St. John's University in May, 1943. Bill was a great athlete but especially skilled at baseball, one of his many true loves. He loved his Church, his parents and his dear wife Mary. Mary was a Gallagher and a Brooklynite. They were married while Bill was a St. John's student. Their only child, William Gary, was born in early '44. Bill talked often of Gary and Mary, as if they were a single true love. Bill was a baseball pitcher. He was superb and at least one year led the Redmen to a baseball championship.

With a wife who was expecting Bill might have had a draft deferment. But he enlisted in the U. S. Army Air Force after graduation and volunteered for combat training. Eventually he was assigned to a B-17 crew and qualified as a bombardier. His crew was in the Eighth Air Force. Bill completed his quota of 25 missions on February 1, 1945. But remember "Catch 22"! The Eighth had raised the quota to 35. Bill received his air medal and a few oak leaf clusters. But he and his crew knew that there would be ten more missions ahead of them before he could head back to Brooklyn and Mary and Gary. They would fly 26 on February 3. Bill's son was just one year old.

Let me digress for a moment. Kriegies had their own lexicon. A new Kriegie's report about the details of his problems with a German fighter plane or with the Jerry flak and his eventual capture by the Germans was referred to as a "horror story." My personal "horror story"—that our plane had been hit on the bomb run, that the number one engine was lost, the prop windmilled and the plane caught fire and eventually exploded and that nine of the ten crew members survived and were captured—was so prosaic that I almost felt ashamed to report what an "easy" time we had.

Logan' s "horror story" was a gem. He was in the lead plane heading down the bomb run when a flak burst got one of the engines. The prop was feathered and prudence dictated that the crew would hook up their chutes. Bill hooked just one buckle so that the chute would dangle to the left of the Norden Bomb sight and give him freedom to sight in on the aiming point. Just as he was yelling "bombs away" the plane exploded.

Most of the crew died. Bill was knocked unconscious by the explosion. His next moment of awareness was a feeling of peace and quiet. As he slowly revived Bill realized that in the explosion the nose of the plane must have disintegrated and he was blown through the opening. Also, the force of the explosion or some other mystic force had popped open the ripcord on his chute and he was drifting down into Germany. I am a scientist who has dealt with probability all of his professional life. I wouldn't begin to assess the probability of Logan's miraculous survival—and I am sure you understand.

The Germans captured Bill shortly after he landed and eventually he wound up in Stalag Luft #3 in Nuremberg. Bill was very popular. Unlike the vast majority of prisoners he was a father. Only a small proportion of Air Force fliers were married in those days. And only a small proportion of married fliers had children. So Bill's references to his "William Gary" warmed many a heart. He epitomized our yearning.

On the morning of April 4 Bill and the hundreds of other Kriegies in Compound 2 got the word—"Be ready to march in an hour." It was 1:30 before we actually walked out the gate. In the meantime we started to form ranks. Bill Logan and his two partners were just ahead of me and Tracy and Stofko. Each group of three were issued a Red Cross parcel. We each received a share of all the cigarettes that were still in the commissary. And each Kriegie was given a large piece of dark yellow laundry soap along with the word that soap would be very valuable for barter during the march. We quickly learned the German equivalent of "bread for soap"—*Brot fur Seife*.

The sun was out and the temperature rose to a comfortable level by noon. So when we actually hit the road we were in a very festive mood. We were leaving the dirt and the bedbugs of Barracks #4 behind. Each of us received one blanket which we examined carefully to make sure it was vermin free before we made a blanket roll pack. We headed west from the site of the Stalag Luft and then swung around toward the south.

The first two hours were a joyous relief from the tether of the barbed wire of the Stalag. Bill Logan started to talk about one of his loves, baseball. He said that St. John's would probably be playing that day and that his beloved Brooklyn Dodgers would play their opener in about a week. I started to think back with fondness about the many Boy Scout hikes I had enjoyed. It was a grand early April day.

At 1:30 we entered a small village named Feucht (meaning moist). We crossed under a very small bridge over which ran a railroad line. Up in the air directly ahead of us we saw a rare sight in those days of dwindling Nazi gasoline. Two FW-190's were zipping along flying east. A cacophony of "boo, boo" rent the air. Then off to the west we could see a squadron of four P-47's (Thunderbolts) giving chase to the FW's. The cry then was "hurrah, hurrah"! Tracy, who was a P-47 pilot, had bragged a lot about this plane. Republic built more than 12,000 of these rugged fighters, more than any fighter before or since. It had a powerful radial engine and was equipped with over a dozen forward-firing .50 caliber machine guns. In addition, it could carry an amazing tonnage of bombs. The Wehrmacht soldiers feared it above all other Allied planes.

Tracy was watching the Thunderbolts very closely and echoed apprehension when the lead plane started rocking. Tracy said "He's looking us over" and then "Those bastards are coming down." Obviously they were mistaking us for a column of German troops. What a tempting target we presented. Bill Logan said aloud "Holy Mary, Mother of God. Pray...." as he headed left off the highway. I am not a Catholic but like Logan I attended a Catholic college so had heard the "Hail Mary" thousands of times. As I headed for the right side of the highway I silently continued Bill's prayer ".. for us sinners now and in the hour of our death...." One of the guards hit the dirt beside me and he was saying "*Unser Vater.*"

For two seconds there was a rat-a-tat of Thunderbolt guns, the explosion of a bomb a few rods away and the unexpected fire from an Ack-ack gun the Germans had hidden by the railroad bridge. Then it was over and a dead silence reigned. The planes did not come in for a second pass, thank God. Across the road I could see the prostrate form of Bill Logan. I ran over to him. He was unconscious and bleeding profusely from a huge tear in his left thigh. To my everlasting shame and remorse I hesitated in removing my white scarf. Tony DeCilis handed me a strip of blanket. I had in my pocket a smooth stone that I used to whet my knife. I placed the stone on the pressure point near the groin just over the spot where the femoral artery nears the surface. I wrapped the strip of blanket around Bill's leg and over the smooth stone. Gerry Gerhardt handed me a small stick and I could complete the tourniquet which I tightened securely. I looked at Bill's face and recalled a line from one of Robert Service's poems, "But God! he looked ghastly pale." I tested his pulse but it was so faint that I wasn't sure it existed.

The guards were yelling at me to get back in the march formation which had reassembled. I stuck with Bill for several minutes when along came a tall, lanky medic POW. He had a few bandages and some morphine. He concurred that the pulse was gone. He said he would take over and I hurried on ahead and eventually joined Stofko and Tracy. About an hour later the lanky medic was hurrying by us and he confirmed that Logan was dead, as I already knew.

Now in early 1991 we are in another war. The sturdy leader of our forces in The Gulf is General Schwarzkopf. He is a good general to lead the troops. Schwarzkopf, himself, was nearly the victim of "friendly fire" when a "hung up" bomb slipped loose from a B-52 over his location in Vietnam. Last week he had this to say: "Any soldier worth his salt should be anti-war. All you have to do is hold your first soldier who is dying in your arms, and have that terribly futile feeling that I can't do anything about it, that life is literally flowing out of this young man and I can't do anything about it. Then you understand the horror of war."

Yes, Bill Logan and Dresden changed my thoughts about war forevermore. Exactly seven months from the day Logan died, Tony DeCilis, Gerry Gehrhart and I met by coincidence at the "Corner" in State College, PA. We three were among the first G.I. Bill-sponsored students to enroll at Penn State after the war ended. For a brief moment we reprised the events of April 4. We never talked about it again.

Almost exactly 45 years after the fateful day I returned to the exact spot where Logan's blood and life ebbed away. Then I visited the small cemetery at Feucht. Near the entrance to this cemetery was an unmarked grave. The rectangular space was delineated with a six inch high masonry wall. The grave was covered with green, green ivy. It was a peaceful spot. An elderly lady who lived in Feucht told me that buried there was *ein Auslander—ein Soldat* [a foreign soldier]. Perhaps that is where Bill's body lies. Today Feucht is well known to the US Air Force. Located there is a large US Air Base. We now protect the Germany we once destroyed. This Air Base may or may not have a name. I choose to think of it as William Logan Field.

✪

CHAPTER 5

THE MARCH TO MOOSBURG

After the harrowing experience of "friendly fire" we were in a somber mood as we marched southward and left the village of Feucht behind. Every few hours we would have a rest (and toilet) break. Colonel Good passed the word that in the event of the return of U.S. fighter aircraft we were to maintain our formation on the highway as a signal that we were not German troops. Also some of the men were given rolls of toilet paper with which to spell P O W at the side of the road if aircraft were sighted. A few hours later a single P-51 approached. The pilot came in low but not on a strafing approach—i.e. he came in at right angles to the line of march—and directly at the head of the column and Colonel Good. The colonel stood his ground and the plane fired no rounds to the relief of all nearby. Now we were sure that we had been recognized and were in less danger of death from "friendly fire."

On we marched and Tracy, Stofko and I agreed on a team strategy that proved to work very well. We were thinking of what to do when the signal to bivouac for the night was announced. Tyler was to hasten to contact the local gentry and barter for food. We pooled our cigarettes and soap, the one standard of exchange we had. Food was the object, of course. Tracy would head out and garner the best supply of wood, which we needed for fuel for the little "Smoky Stover" wood burners we had. Basically a Smoky Stover was a small stove. The base was a Klim can, about the size of a two-pound coffee can. Holes were cut in the bottom. Attached above the hole in the top of the Klim can was a smaller can, about the size of a bean can. A wire grate was inserted between the Klim can and the bean can. It was a very efficient stove. Stofko's role was to find the most comfortable spot for sleeping and to stake out this valued section of ground—or barn or hayloft—if possible. After we had marched another 10 kilometers from Feucht we received the word to bivouac. We were in a wooded section of that part of Germany. I remembered those Boy Scout hikes where we slept overnight without tents. Each of us had a single blanket. We decided to pool our protection. To be fair we would put one blanket on the ground, and have two blankets above and rotated the center position every third night. Lucky Pierre!

Up early. We were on the road again by 8 a.m. The weather was mostly sunny and we made good progress on our southbound route. We were just north of the city of Neumarkt when we found we had a ringside view of a massive US Air Force raid on Nuremberg. We were certain they were pummeling the city to break the resistance just before Patton hit town. The raid lasted for two hours. Bomber formations by the hundreds, mostly B-17's, flew over the remains of the city that was the Nazi birthplace. Wave after wave dropped countless bombs. The sunny sky was crisscrossed with the endless contrails that seemed to persist that day for the longest time. Then there were several vertical smoke markers that marked the specific aiming points. We were about 15 miles south of the targeted areas but the formations were rallying right and many came directly overhead. Despite the fact that there were no military targets near us we were legitimately nervous. Even at this distance we could see cascades of bombs head downward from the planes. We could hear the distant boom-boom, now faint after traveling the 15 miles. There was an even more emphatic signal the bombs left. The concussion sent giant ripples moving along the hundreds of contrails high above us. The awesome power of this giant raid was so much more present when down below than it ever was when up above. Truly Hitler and his *"ein Volk, ein Deutschland"* was reaping the whirlwind. But the bombers started to head back to England and their escorting fighter planes started to roam at lower altitudes. We assembled a few POW signs on the ground—and in a hurry.

We marched on into Neumarkt and wound up at the end of the longest, slowest line I would ever be in during my whole life. At the front of the line it was alleged there would be hot food. First it became cloudy and then it started to rain and turn cooler. The line inched forward interminably. Cold and wet, tired you bet. And thirteen hours of line standing brought Stofko, Tyler and Tracy to the back of the rations truck. They had just <u>run out</u> of soup—and were cutting the bread ration in half. To this day I almost hyperventilate if I stand in line more than a few minutes. Because Patton was so close the Jerries were bound to make up for this long delay in Neumarkt. After we ate our meager meal we were brought into marching formation as darkness fell—and the rain fell—and the cold fell—and our spirits fell. No longer was it a Boy Scout hike. We walked all night. The rain made our clothes and blankets and load that much heavier. Our tender feet in the wet shoes were sore and blistered. On we went. By 3 a.m. we were automatons. Each focused on the moving body just dead ahead. When that body stopped its forward motion a collision was inevitable. From above the line of marchers must have resembled an accordion as we first opened ranks wide and then slammed them closed. At daybreak we were allowed to stop for a few hours and eat a small breakfast. Somebody scrounged some dead wood, probably a farm fence, and we built a fire and warmed our hands and our butts.

Then on again and more rain. The next village we encountered was Berching. This was an ancient place, still surrounded entirely by a thick high wall. The wall was built in Roman times to help in the constant repulsion of the Goths from the north. We stood in line again for a long time but today there was a Red Cross parcel for the three amigos. We ate a good meal and then slept wet and miserable in a dirty small barn near the village of Beilngries. The next day, April 7, was clear and warm—and <u>no marching</u>. There was a creek nearby so we could wash and then dry our clothes and our feet. Happiness is such a relative thing. We were never so pleased or more content than for such simple luxuries. Our trading for food was very successful too. The men wanted cigarettes and the women wanted soap. In trade we got lots of potatoes, some better farm bread and above all, a few eggs. That evening we enjoyed a real repast. And Tracy located a good hay mow for sleeping. Ah, joy, joy, joy!

Early morning, April 8: with spirits renewed, we hiked on, and on, and on, and on. By afternoon we had 30 kilometers behind us and we were just north of the Danube river. Before we crossed the bridge over the Danube we were given very strict orders to keep moving, once we were on the bridge. The reason was apparent.

The German engineers had wired the bridge to be blown when we and the other Kriegies had crossed. We obeyed orders, keeping our heads high and our marching steady until we were on the other side. We were nervous for another reason, too. The "heavies" were out again in force. We were crossing the Danube just north of the city of Neustadt. This is located about halfway between the cities of Regensburg and Ingolstadt. Both of these cities were targets that day. Another target appeared to be a much smaller city, Donaauworth, just west of Ingolstadt. We were running out of good targets if we were bombing small cities like Donauworth. With these three targets nearby the bomber formations were crossing overhead from what seemed all directions—for almost an hour. We breathed easier when the bombers headed west and the fighter escort planes put on a little show of aerial acrobatics for us. They convinced us their message was "We recognize you as POWs."

The next several days were almost a delight. The weather was friendly and the section of Germany we had entered was Bavaria. It was a rural area and seemed untouched by the war. The small villages we "invaded" saw in us more of the war than they had experienced to date. With all the fresh air and exercise and better diet we were looking fit—but dirty and unkempt. Thornton and Narracci were near to us, but the enlisted men were further behind in the line of march. Narracci had developed a deep tan that enhanced his rugged good looks. Thornton talked longingly of home in California. We all thought more of home now, because the war news was daily more encouraging.

Nuremberg had fallen so Patton was hot on our heels. We had learned that our destination was a large infantry prison camp, a *Stammlager,* numbered VII-A, in the city of Moosburg just north and east of Munich. We were thankful for two reasons: one, that it was only twenty miles away, and two, we were not destined for Dachau, also just north, but a little west of Munich. The German guards were all old men who could hardly wait for the war to end. They would smile and say "Soon we will be your prisoners." When asked about Dachau they were reticent to speak—would say only that it was reserved for "political" prisoners, the Jerry euphemism for *die Jude*.

Bavaria was very picturesque and beautiful. It is a Catholic sector of Germany and many wayside shrines had been built just off the edge of the roads. More than one Kriegie knelt and offered a prayer at these roadside shrines. How Bill Logan would have been pleased to see this symbol of the Christian face of Germany. We were astounded to see our first hops farm. Hops grow as vines that are thirty feet long. On the hops farms are gigantic hops vines ladders built of long, long poles, thinner but as long as a telephone pole. It would be another month before the vines would begin their growing season. When I returned to this line of march 45 years later it was May and the hops farms were still in the same place and the vines were already ten feet high at that time of year.

The villages of Rommelsdorf, and Mulhausen and Schweinbach were on our line of march. At each village the guards never objected if we broke ranks occasionally to barter with one of the villagers. Fortunately we would get a Red Cross parcel once in a while. This replenished my supply of cigarettes, the universal medium of exchange then and for at least another year after the war ended.

Maybe we should have expected some bad news on Friday the thirteenth. But early in the morning the news swept up and down the column that President Roosevelt had died the evening before. Mostly we were soldiers, not Republicans or Democrats. Most were not old enough to have ever voted. For all of us Roosevelt was the only president we had ever known. I was the old man of the crew and I was only 12 when Roosevelt started his reign. He was not just the president—he was the Commander in Chief. He was the father figure who had led us into war and through the battles and to the wondrous victory all but within his grasp. We truly mourned. Ten thousand Kriegies formed the first and longest of the many funeral corteges in his honor.

I grew up surrounded by Republicans. Grandpa Tyler was so ardent a follower that he could barely say the words Democrat or Roosevelt aloud. But I had spent four years at a Catholic school, the University of Scranton. There I was surrounded by Irish Democrats' sons and sons of liberal Jewish families. I was exactly 21 years old on election day in 1940. I voted for Wendell Willkie. I am proud of that vote. Lincoln, the greatest liberal of the previous century, was the first Republican president. How times change! Willkie was the last liberal Republican candidate for the presidency, and was a great man. His book, "One World," is more than ever worth reading today. In the election of 1944 I voted for Roosevelt. I am proud of that vote, too. Roosevelt was truly the Giant in the United States during the first half of the 20th century. Yes, the 13th of April was a black Friday for the Kriegies.

The Kriegies ahead of us had already reached Moosburg. The Germans, even as disaster entombed them, were continuing to be precise and orderly. Each of the thousands of Kriegies had to be processed, counted and assigned to a new compound and barracks—or tent. So the line slowed down. We covered only 15 miles in the last week—through Holzhausen, Obermunchen, Reichensdorf and then to Moosburg and Stalag Luft 7-A on April 20. By the time I reached Moosburg I looked like a "bag lady." For one thing, to keep my head warm I had cut a 16-inch section from one of the sleeves of my "Long Johns," tied the narrow end with some string and stretched the wider end to fit over my head and ears. Along the way I had scrounged a 6- or 7-foot length of very large diameter wire. I had bent this so it could be set on the ground and used as a grate for cooking. To carry it I slipped it over my hips and tied the open side with a rope across my belly. From this sooty wire grate around my middle I dangled an assortment of tin cans that we used as cooking utensils. Occasionally I would get a reflection of myself, and was reminded of the cartoon character, "Happy Hooligan."

Before being assigned to a barracks each of us had a few minutes in a warm shower. Another little joy in life. Stofko and Tracy were in my barracks and Rury, Thornton and Narracci were nearby. But, the enlisted men on the crew were not readily accessible. I missed the frequent bull sessions I had had with Yovich, our tail gunner. There were two fairly distinguished Kriegies in my barracks. One was Col. Clark, the son of General Mark Clark, who commanded the Fifth Army in its mudslogging trek and battle up the boot of Italy. The other notable was Capt. John Winant Jr., the son of the Ambassador to St. James. Captain Carlsen was still my "boss" and Tony DeCilis, my first aid partner in trying to staunch the life blood ebbing from Bill Logan two weeks before, had the bunk below me.

Stalag Luft VII-A was vastly overcrowded—at least 20,000 prisoners in an area designed for 5,000. And it was a polyglot mix. There were infantry and Air Force, French and English, Serbs and Russians. Most of the Serbs were old and grizzled. They had been prisoners for several years. They hated the Germans with a passion the Americans never displayed. There was a not very defensible fence between us and the old Serbs. That only served as a bartering wall for trading cigarettes for the pots and pans that the Serbs crafted from old tin cans. I even got a proper knife that one of the Serbs had fashioned from scraps of metal. The Russians were more sullen than the other prisoners. But all of us could sense that liberation was near at hand.

Sunday, April 29, was *der tag*. We awoke early, anticipating our hour of liberation. All of the Germans were gone. The sounds of battle were imminent, only a mile or so northwest of the camp. At first we climbed on the roofs of the barracks to get a good view of the fireworks, but the sound of bullets whizzing nearby sent us scurrying for cover. The battle focused on the city of Moosburg, just south of the Stalag. By noon the battle was over and the first one of the great Sherman tanks of the 14th Armored Division rolled into camp. Within moments the American flag was hoisted aloft over Stalag Luft VII-A. At first the flag was upside down but was lowered and sent aloft with the 48 stars in the upper left quadrant. For all the Kriegies this was the sweetest moment of the war. In later years some Americans chose to burn this flag. The great song writer, Tom T. Hall, put it best, "I know you burned your flag, but I'm sure glad you couldn't burn mine. My flag flies in my heart. My flag flies in my mind." Today, I never see that flag without seeing in my mind the unfurling of "Old Glory" that Sunday in Stalag Luft *Sieben Ah*.

A few hours later down a cleared corridor in center camp came another beautiful sight. Five Jeeps in tandem rolled in. It was General George Patton and his entourage. He stood up on the Jeep and addressed us and called us heroes. He was resplendent in battle jacket, polished helmet and ivory-handled pistols. For us he was the great liberator.

At exactly the moment that the flag was raised over Moosburg an event occurred two hundred miles to the northwest. A mad dictator raised a pistol and fired a fatal bullet into his brain. Now both Roosevelt and Hitler were dead. These two leaders of implacable enemies came to power the same year—in early 1933. Hitler espoused fascism and met the fate that fascists deserve. His grand proclamation of a "*ein tausend Jahre Reich*" was short 988 years. Roosevelt fought fascism with all the power of his crippled body, his strong voice and his monumental spirit. There was never a question about who wore the "white hat."

CHAPTER 6

✪

RECOVERED ALLIED MILITARY PERSONNEL

Thus, that marvellous last Sunday in April saw the end for us of being *Kriegies* and the beginning for us of being RAMP's (Recovered Allied Military Personnel). We were free again. We will never forget those first sights of freedom... the flag unfurling, the huge General Sherman tank with its long powerful cannon breaching the barbed wire, the sight of a Jeep again and the appearance of an L-5 (Piper Cub) buzzing the camp. All served full notice that our days as POWs were ended.

We were even free of military discipline for awhile. Some of the more adventuresome left the area and walked and hitchhiked their way to such glamour spots as Cannes and Nice before returning to military control.

Most of us were content to follow the "suggestion" of Col. Good that we "stay put and await transportation." We were told that we would have top priority for return to the States. It was a double-edged sword that would give us early severance from Europe. Sure, we had been POWs, but we were well trained airmen who could be reassigned in what we thought would be a long air battle with the hated Japanese. So there was apprehension as well as joy in going home.

At first the senior officers wanted to restrict us to camp, but the temptation to roam could not be resisted for long. April 30 was the first full day back in the Army—not too different from the preceding few. Off to the south the sounds of battle receded with the promise of carrying the war away from us forever. On

May 1 it snowed. The Russians celebrated this May Day all day in song and dance and mini parades. They were joyous knowing that Hitler was dead and that their soldiers had occupied Berlin. We were ill prepared for the snow and cold but a lot of little things kept reminding us that no Jerrysonofabitch had any say-so now. For one thing we saw a Red Cross *girl*. She came in to camp in her Red Cross wagon and doled out hot coffee and *doughnuts*. And most wonderful of all for us food-starved ex-Kriegies was the fact that we had some fresh white bread for the evening meal. No cake will ever taste better.

The next day Stofko and I went into the city, only a half mile south of the camp. We discovered soon that hundreds of ex-POWs had "liberated" every chicken and pig within fifty miles. But we hit a bonanza. In one building we entered there were a half dozen Italian soldiers. They had once been the allies of Germany but had been treated as semi-prisoners since Italy surrendered. We poked around in one of their closets and discovered a whole crate of fresh eggs. They must have been laid by Nazi chickens since each was labeled with a tiny German eagle—similar to our own NRA eagle that was seen everywhere in the mid thirties, but never on eggs—even those laid by Democrat chickens. We gave the Italians a few cigarettes and stuffed our jackets with all the eggs we could carry safely. Next we entered what was quite like a small dormitory. There were about twenty young ladies quartered there. Almost all had the same story—they had lived in a city that had been bombed so their parents sent them to this small city which was an unlikely target. They all worked in a small fertilizer plant in Moosburg. Their food supply was limited, too, so they were delighted when we began to unload the plentiful supply of eggs from our flight jackets. Then they fixed for me and Stofko the best meal since that long ago day when I ate my last meal before the final mission. Like that meal it was eggs and pancakes—but what pancakes. They were thin and light and tender and large. They were served rolled like a jelly cake. On top of each of these treats was a faint sprinkling of powdered sugar—probably the last the girls had. Oh, culinary heaven .. oh, divine repast! Once again I blessed Brother Timothy for teaching me the rudiments of the German language. Talking to these beautiful girls was also a delicate treat. Later, back in camp we told no one about either the eggs or the girls. Now that we were free we tended to stop sharing—a "civilization" syndrome. But that day I remember an incident that in an eye blink revealed that prison life had subdued some sensibilities. I was in the top bunk watching Tony DeCilis spread a slice of his white bread with some oleo. He dropped his knife on the dirty floor and without a reservation picked it up and wiped it on the trouser part covering his thigh. But his trousers were revoltingly filthy with months of grime and oil and soil imbedded—much worse than the dirty floor. He proceeded with his meal as if the butler had just laid out the best silver.

Meanwhile back in the USA the ten families of the ten members of our crew on that fateful Ides of March received a third official letter from the Air Force. It was a good news—bad news letter. The good news was the enclosure of a list of the ten mailing addresses of the next of kin of each crew member. The bad news from the stupid Major Reed who wrote the letter was in a very disturbing and <u>completely inappropriate</u> paragraph......

This is what my mother read in the letter from Foggybottom:

"Additional information has been received indicating that Lt. Tyler was the navigator on a B-17 (Flying Fortress) bomber which departed from Italy on a bombardment mission to Ruhland, Germany on 15 March 1945. The missing plane report reveals that during this mission abut 2:15 p.m., over Bautzen, Germany, our planes were subjected to enemy antiaircraft fire and your son's bomber sustained damage. Subsequently the disabled craft began to lose altitude, <u>fell into a spin</u>, and disappeared from view. Inasmuch as the crew members of accompanying planes were unable to obtain any other details relative to the loss of this aircraft, the foregoing constitutes all the information presently available."

Two days later my mother received a nice note from Lucille Thornton.

"I know that you are deeply troubled by the sad news concerning your son, Lt. Leslie Tyler. My husband, Lt. Dale Thornton, was piloting the ship your son was on, March 15th last. I have never for one minute given the crew up—they are just temporarily out of direct contact with us. I think, without a doubt, that we should all keep in touch with each other. One of us might hear from some one of the crew members, either directly or indirectly.

Mrs. Tyler, if there are any details which you do not have and which you think I might have, please do not hesitate to write me. Again let me say that I am confident we will hear from the crew very soon.

Sincerely,
Lucille Thornton

That same day (May 1) I was able to get my hands on a blank sheet of V-Mail and wrote a short letter home. I would almost beat that letter to Scranton, however.

A week later my mother received a second welcome and reassuring letter from Lucille:

Dear Mrs. Tyler,
Received your lovely letter of May 1st & I hasten to give you what bit of information I have.
I too received the word that the plane "fell into a spin"—but that is much different than the other reports I have received that I am not putting too much faith in it.
Fortunately, I have some very close friends who witnessed the boys' plane & here is what I am told. A friend of my husband just returned from over there. His last raid happened to be on the same one as Dale and Leslie. Dale has been Squadron Leader for some time now & was such on this particular raid. His plane was spotted easily because his ship had the RADAR. Dale ra-

dioed the flight after being hit that he was heading for
Russian territory & all 4 motors were running and no
smoke was coming from the plane. This Captain is of
the opinion, of course he doesn't know, that his oxygen
tanks were hit and of course, he would have to come
down to live. He was 75 miles South of Berlin & 30 miles
West of the Russian front.

I also received the same report from a photographer
who went over the Target one hour after our boys. He
was kind enough to go to Dale's headquarters & get this
same information for me. Information, which, of
course, the Army will not give out. I also talked with a
lieutenant at the A.A.F. headquarters today and he said
that had Dale crashed and been killed in either Russia or
Germany that I would, of course, know by this time.

I am very hopeful & have never at any time given
them up. You may be sure that I will wire you immediately, should anything arrive, telling of their where-
abouts.

Thanks so much for writing. That was so thoughtful
of you.

Sincerely,
Lucille Thornton

We were to stay in the old Moosburg camp as RAMPs for
only a week. We had no duty assignments so we roamed further
and further from Moosburg on foot. This Bavarian sector of
Germany was delightful as the new crops turned the fields
green and here and there was a huge field of bright yellow mustard. A few of the fruit trees were in blossom and there in this
peaceful setting the war seemed more like a dream. But we
heard, too, of a real nightmare. Several of the RAMPs had hiked
the few miles to visit the infamous Death Camp at Dachau. They
returned with stories of this worst ever of human obscenities.
These grim and grotesque tales reemphasized the monstrosity of
the evil against which we had fought. We were reminded anew
about the Frank Capra movies that were part of our early Army

indoctrination. These movies were a marvelous series and were titled "Why we Fight." Now we knew too, that the title should be "Why We Must Win!"

Speaking of movies—Stofko and I found a small contingent of tank repair specialists who set up shop nearby. Each evening they showed another movie. We saw two of them. One was another John Wayne classic, called "Tall In the Saddle." Another was one of the familiar "Thin Man" fine films.

The Army trucks started to arrive to move us out. On May 8 Stofko and I were at the front of the line. Our truck ride ended at an airfield adjacent to the city of Ingolstadt on the Danube (This is where the Audi automobiles are now manufactured). Shortly after we got to Ingolstadt we heard a radio message that Churchill had announced that the war in Europe was officially over. For us this V-E day was anticlimactic. Our own V-E Day would ever be April 29, the day Patton liberated Moosburg. Just after the VE pronouncement I heard what would be my last angry sounds of war. A German plane, a JU-87, came in to the airport to surrender to the Americans rather than to the Russians. The German pilot made the mistake of not landing on the first pass (probably wanted a view of the runway for bomb craters.) When he leveled off at about 50 feet all kinds of Ack-ack fire materialized. The accompanying tracer bullets made it look like a fireworks display. Fortunately the plane was not destroyed and the pilot brought it around and landed. The RAMPs swarmed over the plane and dismantled it for souvenirs.

Speaking of souvenirs, that night we went over to an old *Wehrmacht* warehouse to sleep inside. And when we left we carried off a variety of German war gear. I carried home a helmet and two bayonets and two saddle bags. There were over a thousand pairs of beautiful skis that were a temptation— but obviously too awkward to carry.

On May 10 it was my turn to board a C-47, fly west and end my not-quite two months' stay in war-torn Germany. My last memorable sight of that defeated country was a 1,000-foot altitude slow turn view of Stuttgart. This city had been pounded from the air for almost five years. The low altitude view from the C-47 froze in my mind the finality of the vanquished Reich.

This pummeled, almost powdered remnant of a grand and beautiful city resembled the end of the war attitude of the proud and awful people who stormed into Poland six years before. They were demolished as well as vanquished. Today there are still some proud and haughty Germans. But the warrior nation of Bismarck and Wilhelm and Hitler has disappeared.

From Stuttgart the marvelous aircraft headed further west and landed at Rheims, where the Germany surrender documents had been signed a few days earlier. In one of my Dunmore grade school geography books was a favorite picture of mine. It depicted the lovely "Cathedral of Rheims." When we rode past this magnificent structure it was like a dream of mine fulfilled.

We stayed at Rheims just one night. In the morning we stripped the foul and filthy garments we wore. Onto the pile they went to be exorcised from this life forever. We were issued clean underwear and clean fatigues, socks and new shoes. Then it was on to the ubiquitous Army trucks for a long, long ride almost to the English Channel. Our ride ended at a huge tent city called Camp Lucky Strike. In all these moves I became separated from Stofko, and in fact from all the other crew members, most of whom I have never seen again.

At Lucky Strike we were issued a full dress uniform. I felt resplendent with my navigator wings, silver bars and the Air Medal ribbon, complete with the oak leaf cluster. But we were dismayed to learn that we would not be paid until we returned to the US. And, believe it or not, that turned out to be "no problem." Each day we could claim rations of "goodies" at the PX. I built up a supply of cartons of cigarettes and candy bars. When I had enough of this loot and was convinced it would be several days before we would leave France I packed up my loot and headed for Paris. "How are you going to keep them down on the farm after...?"

My three days in Paris are a memory to be savored. People who go there now can't believe that there were no taxis, or any civilian vehicles, on the streets of Paris. There were a few Jeeps and trucks for hitchhiking and the Metro was fully operational. It was easy to get all around the city on this subway network. I climbed the Eiffel Tower, was respectfully subdued in the quiet of the Sacred Heart and Notre Dame Cathedrals. I marched under the Arch of Triumph and ogled the pretty girls on their bicycles as I sipped absinthe on the Champs Elysees. The second day I got a ride out to Versailles and the Hall of Mirrors. In a sense this is where World War II started when Lloyd George and Clemenceau battered down the idealistic Wilson—and gave Hitler the cause he could sell to the German people.

One night I went to the "Follies." Instead of baldheaded men the overstuffed chairs in the first two rows were filled with young U.S Army lieutenants, me included. I tried to track down my best friend from the University of Scranton, Donald (now a Captain) Reap. No luck on that. But I did team up with two young officers who had been classmates of mine at the Meteorology School in Grand Rapids, Mich. earlier in the war. I could brag to them that I was the only meteorologist in the history of warfare to be captured by the enemy.

All of the French civilians, especially the girls, were more than generous to all of the U.S. military, whom they viewed as the saviors of France. Thus, I could spend the three days in Paris without using up my complete supply of cigarettes. They were better than money. But good things end and it was back to Camp Lucky Strike.

While I was in Paris the last official messages from Air Force were being sent to describe the finish of the saga of Thornton's crew. My mother received this telegram:

PA157 20 GOVT=WUX WASHINGTON DC 16 MAY 1109 A
MRS FREDA H TYLER=
981 RICHTER ST SCRANTON PENN=
THE SECRETARY OF WAR DESIRES ME TO INFORM YOU
THAT YOUR SON 1/LT TYLER LESLIE J RETURNED TO MILI-
TARY CONTROL=
ULIO THE ADJUTANT GENERAL.

1/LT

Shortly thereafter my mother heard from that most considerate lady, Mrs. Dale Thornton:

May 24, '45

Dear Mrs. Tyler,
        Received word from the Red Cross today that Dale
had been liberated. I need not tell you how pleased I am.
        I sincerely hope that you have received the same
good news from Leslie. If you haven't already heard you
undoubtedly will.
        Please let me hear from you again soon, regarding
Lester.

Sincerely,
Lucille Thornton

        My mother had written to the families of the other nine
crew members after the mid-May telegram. Sandy's grand-
mother was the only respondent without a "good news" message to report.

        2214 N. Collins
        Lockport, Ill.
        May 28, 1945
        Mrs. Freda H. Tyler

Dear Mrs. Tyler,
        I am very happy to hear the news you received
about your son.
        As yet we haven't had any news about my grandson,
T/Sgt. Sator Sanchez. But I'm not giving up hope. And, I
hope it won't be long before I will get the good news
too. Thank you for letting me know. I had a letter from
Mrs. Dale Thornton telling me about her husband.

Sincerely,
Mrs. Belen Sanchez

        Back at Lucky Strike an event brightened a few of the re-
maining days. One of the RAMPs in my tent was Lt. Jensen. He

claimed to have been a Kriegie longer than any other infantry soldier. He was in the first wave to storm ashore in North Africa in the invasion in '42. That was the infantry's first taste of battle in the ETO in WWII. Jensen was captured a few minutes after he hit the beach, half drowned and defenseless. He talked often of his fiancee, who happened to be in the Army, too. She was a nurse and wrote to him often in the long and many months he was a Kriegie. It turned out that at that very time she was in France. She was obviously a very determined young lady. She pestered all the SHAEF officers she could until she learned that Jensen was now a RAMP and was located at Camp Lucky Strike. What a reunion that was for Jensen when his wife to be came in to our tent. Within the hour they decided to get married that very day. All his buddies in our tent hiked with the two of them to the small village of Pourville nearby. We sought out the mayor of the village and he performed the ceremony in French. Several of the local gentry caught the festive spirit and it was a joyous affair, complete with a champagne toast over and over for the bride and groom. The mayor even arranged for the use of the town castle for the wedding night. What a grand reality that day was for all of us. Not only was the war over, but "life goes on."

It was a year from D-Day on June 6 that we were scheduled for departure. We left Camp Lucky Strike, and Dieppe, where so many Canadians met death on the abortive commando raid on March 28, 1942, a grim and gory disaster. On we went to the port of Le Havre, the scene of one of the great victories just after D-Day. We boarded the ship, a converted freighter, named the U.S.S. Explorer. It was a 15,000 tonner, but we drew quarters in the bow and it was dank and dark and rough up there. Still, we were on the way home. It was only a 12 day journey, but to all of us it seemed like it took twice as long as it should., The best feature of the trip back was the opportunity to eat three meals a day from china and silver and eat all we wanted of good, good, good American chow. We sailed on and on and were disappointed to learn three days out that we would not go to New York City as scheduled. How we longed to see "The Lady," that emblem of for what we fought, that beacon of liberty for the oppressed, that symbol of the part of America that is still good.

On June 21, the summer solstice of what may be humankind's most fateful year, we arrived at the very port from which we sailed a long, long eight months before. We disembarked at Hampton Roads, Virginia. It was good to see America again. Yes, it was good to see America again. Once ashore we were allowed to make a long distance phone call. My family was well and were going to await my arrival at Philadelphia. After the phone calls we took the train to that peaceful spot, Camp Patrick Henry. Then it was on to Fort Dix, the entry spot for so many GIs. We were delighted at the efficiency there. In 24 hours we were processed—assigned to a unit so that we could get all that back pay, get a new ID card and be given orders for TDY at home for sixty days. My sister, who was a U.S. Navy WAVE, and stationed in Washington, D.C., joined my mother, my mother's sisters and me for a glorious reunion in Philadelphia. And the entire sixty days were glorious in many other ways, capped, of course, by the rousing, roaring, magnificent celebration of V-J Day and the end, hopefully, of the last World War. For if there is another, it most surely will be the last.

✪

CHAPTER 7

HONDO FORTY-FOUR FOUR FOUR
NAVIGATORS ALL

"Biloxi Blues." I claim a legitimate authority to use this phrase. I was in Biloxi years before Neil Simon. And I was, while there, much bluer than he. My sad story: I think it started on my eighth birthday when my father took me to the Bijou Theatre in Salamanca to see that marvelous WWI film, "Wings." A young and handsome Buddy Rogers played the lead and for 105 seconds there appeared on screen for the first time a hauntingly impelling new actor, Gary Cooper. This silent film displayed the lyrical scenes of flimsy craft soaring and diving in the chivalrous air warfare of the first great war. This film had the same visceral impact on me then as did that best of all WWII poems, John Gillespie Magee's "High Flight" sonnet, when Bill Dowey read it to me for the first time many years later.

My love of flying grew a notch each time that dad took me to the county fairs in Pennsylvania to see the barnstormers perform. In those depression years we never seemed to be able to afford the few dollars required for the two of us to fly together on the short flights the pilots offered to the public as a source of income. But in a later glorious summer, that of 1940, I learned to fly. Roosevelt's foresight that the United States would very soon be in the huge conflict raging in Europe that year led to the Civilian Pilot Training (CPT) program. Good ol' boy Texan, Dr. Joseph Harper, taught the ground school course at the University of Scranton and Mark Richards was my flight instructor in those little two-seater Piper Cubs. What a thrill to solo for the first time and do those spins over the Scranton Country Club golf course. Ah, yes! Glorious was the word for that summer. But, I grieve still that I never took my dad for a ride in one of those little Cubs. He died flightless the next year.

In the next year came Pearl Harbor and into the conflict we plunged. How that incident changed the lives of the hundred boys who were seniors in the University of Scranton on that fateful day. Most of us had been against involvement prior to December 7, but not one of the hundred would shirk getting directly involved in some way. Since I was one of 20 Pre-med students I had one easy choice. Before graduation we knew that we could apply for medical school acceptance, be accepted and then join the Army or Navy and be sent to Medical School with the military paying the bills and paying us a private's salary. Most of the 20 chose this path. Only three of the 20 would see combat in the war, big Ed Smith, who joined the Navy, stoic Matt Lynott, who became the prototype Marine Corps lieutenant, and L.J.T.

Just before graduation I enlisted in the U.S. Army Air Corps as a "Flying Cadet." It would be four months before I would be called. In those days in order to enlist in this program it was not necessary to pass first the rigorous "six-four" physical exam. However, it was necessary to pass a mental exam, sort of an IQ test for potential pilots. I had been honing for this exam for years, and made such a high score that the Army investigated me through contacts with the faculty at the University of Scranton to make sure that I had not "cheated." When informed by Registrar Frank O'Hara that I was a top honor student they ceased the inquiry and accepted my enlistment on June 6, exactly two years before what will always be known as D-Day.

That summer of '42 I worked at a boy's summer camp, then worked for two months on the Erie Railroad, outside and doing physical labor ($.45 per hour). After work I would walk the two miles to the YMCA and "work out" for an hour. I was in the best shape that I would ever be, and certain I would pass the upcoming 64 Physical. On my birthday, November 2, I received a telegram that I would go on active duty on November 11. So that Armistice Day I and 30 other aspiring pilots convened at the Aviation Cadet Examining Board in Wilkes-Barre prepared for shipment to the Army Air Forces Classification Center in Nashville. We learned forthwith that there is the "right," way, the "wrong" way and the "Army" way. Nashville is south of Wilkes-Barre so we headed north. By nightfall we were in Buffalo and in the midst of a raging snowstorm. Where is sunny Tennessee? The taxis were supposed to take us across town to the L&N Railroad terminal, but could not move in the heavy snow. The noncom in charge was enterprising, though. He contacted Greyhound and got a multi-wheeled bus to get us there on time. Then we headed south to Nashville.

The cadet center was a miserable place. The site was cold, wet, muddy, yet dusty, all the time. We were quartered in tarpaper barracks with a single soft coal-burning stove in the center—putting out more foul smoke and odors than heat. But the excitement of going into flight training and the camaraderie of new friends kept our spirits high. For the most part we were the victims of the hundreds of medical personnel that were the core of the NAAFCC primary activity. First came the "shots." One cadet, after a day of shots in the arm said "It didn't bother me," and proceeded to do 100 push ups. He couldn't make it out of his bunk except for latrine calls all the next day or maybe two. Mostly we were in lines for X-rays, blood pressure measurements, and a whole host of different eye exams. One by one I was passing each of the requirements. Each day a few cadets in the barracks failed a test. That ended their testing and they soon had orders to go elsewhere. After I had passed all the physical tests, there was a fairly short interview with one of the psychologists. We thought this was for the purpose of detecting the few candidates who should be sent to navigation or bombardier training instead of to the desired pilot school. How naive I was! Partway through the interview the psychologist asked me "What sort of things are you afraid of?" I promptly responded that "I am afraid of dogs." I knew I had made a grave error when he started to make copious notes in his notebook. That was it—finis! The next day I received notice that I had failed my ARMA—aptitude required for military aviation. A year does not go by that I still wish that I could have taken that sonofabitch doctor down one of the many bomb runs I made—especially the double on Christmas day, 1944, over the big B, Brux. Maybe he was ashamed of being afraid of dogs—or something.

My buddies in Nashville went on to primary pilot training and I went to Biloxi—to join all those draftees. Yes, I was blue, blue, blue. I spent the first of my Army Christmases on KP in Biloxi as I and the draftees suffered basic training. I spent my first New Year's Eve on KP in Biloxi—still quarantined to the base. My only favorable remembrance of Biloxi was the PA blaring of that great song by Bing Crosby, "White Christmas," the first Christmas it was ever played. And, there I was a short distance from New Orleans—and never made it. In fact, I have yet to visit that city.

But just after the holiday I got some good news. My orders arrived, sending me to meteorology training. When I failed my ARMA in Nashville I was demoted from cadet to private. To study meteorology I was ordained as a cadet once again—but with a difference. I was now a *ground school cadet.* Three of the other graduates in my U of S class had enlisted in this program of meteorology. I knew that the cadets trained at such schools as NYU, California Institute of Technology, MIT, and the University of Chicago. My orders called for me to go to Grand Rapids, Michigan. What University was there? I soon discovered I was part of a fabulous experiment in training weathermen. The Army Air Force had determined that they would need two thousand weather officers in the coming year. The schools I mentioned could supply about 150. The Air Force Training Command was nothing short of miraculous. They decided to take over the hotels and Civic Auditorium in Grand Rapids and train 2000 or more meteorologists before the program ended.

It was a grueling nine months grind, far tougher than my four pre-med years. I was never happy there, dreaming daily about how I might have outfoxed that damn psychologist. But I accepted the program and did fairly well. There were seven other cadets in my room, room 625 of the Pantlind Hotel. There were several hundred cadets in the program. We really filled the Civic Auditorium, which was set up as a laboratory and classroom. Will any of us ever forget Athelstan Spuehlhaus, who taught us dynamic meteorology or Harry Wexler, who taught us practical meteorology? Then there was Col. Lewis, the commandant of cadets. He was a West Pointer and was a tough old soldier—but found it impossible to make us wimpy weathermen into tough soldiers. His boss was Col. MacNeal. Unlike Lewis, he did not have the respect of the cadets.

It was imperative to be friends with the other roommates in order to survive the nine months of gestation. I liked them all. My favorite was cadet Christopher. He was in the top bunk above me. I never slept in my bunk. I made it to pass the inspection, with a flat surface and square corners, and slept on the floor. I always passed the inspection. Upham was a funny character. He did all the dirty jobs to make our room pass the CS inspections. Dunn was a peppy little oldster—much of the faker—but kept up the spirits of the eight. Crego was the little fatty, who had a good sense of humor and a pleasant chuckle. McQuain was an unreconstructed Southerner from West By God Virginia. He was the perpetual rebel. Caracino was somewhat lazy but made good grades and always managed to be in excellent physical shape. Kalbach was young in more than one way. He was impetuous but likeable and did a lot of growing up in the nine months. Cadet William Shea was our burden.

We were confined to quarters so much that the Hotel Pantlind is remembered more as a palatial jail than an army home for nine months. There were three squadrons of cadets, organized by height. The first squadron were the giants, the six-footers. All of us on the sixth floor were in the third squadron, the five-footers. When we marched the big guys set the marching step length. We in the Third could never keep up. We were affectionately known as the "bouncing third." We studied hard for the nine months and watched the war unfold. I was especially interested in the furious battles in the skies above Germany as the 8th Air Force fought its way into the history books. There were our first victories against the Japanese and the Germans. We ousted Rommel from Africa and then from Sicily. The invasion of Italy was raging when we graduated in early September, 1943. Now we were second lieutenants and were sent to assignments all over the world.

My first assignment was a delight. It was Hammer Field in Fresno, California. The weather was marvellous and easy to forecast. Hammer Field was the training site of a new type of modified B-25 twin-engined bombers. This version had a 75mm cannon sticking out its forward fuselage. It would be a power-house against the Japanese supply ships and troop transports. I flew in the 25 every chance I got. It was a rugged bomber and the pilots loved it. But, God, it was noisy. I loved to get in the tail gunner's spot and look out through that bubble of Plexiglas at the orange and almond groves and the endless grape vines of the San Joaquin Valley.

Then there was Mary Jo. We dated as frequently as I could get off the base, which was several times a week. The California life was a revelation. I was now an officer and well paid. For the first time in my life I had money in my pocket. I vowed never again to be without it. Mary Jo and I continued our gentle and warm romance for a month and I awaited an impending assignment that would take me overseas.

Then came my reprieve. I was on duty at the weather station on the midnight shift when in on the telex came a message: THE AIR FORCE TRAINING COMMAND IS SEEKING SEVERAL VOL-UNTEERS FROM THE SEPTEMBER 6 GRADUATION CLASS OF METEOROLOGISTS TO BE GIVEN FLIGHT TRAINING AS NAVI-GATORS. I didn't even check with my boss, Captain Moore. I had my application for this exciting assignment on the return telex within the hour.

My orders arrived. On my birthday, exactly one year from my induction message I was going to get back into flight train-ing. This time I would know what to say to the psychologist (I love dogs). First, Mary Jo and I said our tearful and affectionate farewells. I would never see her again. It was home to Scranton for a few days and then on to Hondo Air Base and the Naviga-tion School there. Hondo is located 40 miles west of San Anto-nio—and there ain't nothing west of San Antonio. I was one of a dozen officers, all lieutenants, who were in class Hondo Forty-four Four Four. This would be the fourth class to graduate in 1944 and we were in the fourth classroom group. Most of the officers were recent graduates of the meteorology class and had volunteered for flight training as had I. There were also in the classroom group about an equal number of aviation cadets. We officers lived in the BOQ (bachelor officer quarters). This sounds great but, in fact, the buildings were tarpaper barracks– a Spartan design for Spartan living. My roommate was John E. Kushner. "Kush" and I clicked. He had a very fine and subtle sense of humor, droll and dry–and he looked the part. He made me laugh often. Kush was a good athlete, strong and wiry and determined. He loved baseball, and said often he wished he were a little better at it so he could feel like he had a shot at the majors.

We rarely played any baseball at Hondo, but we did play touch football almost every day. Part of the training for the cadets was a two-hour PT program–mostly boring calisthenics. The ten officers in the class were exempt from the calisthenics, but were "requested" by Captain Long, the officer in charge of Class Forty-four Four Four, to put in at least an hour a day on some kind of physical activity while the cadets were "calisthenicizing." Touch football rapidly brought out the instinctive leadership qualities in the players. From the first day it was a match between First Lt. Michaels, who had transferred from Army Infantry to Navigation training, and Lt. Davis, a newly trained meteorologist from the area around Boston. The two were usually opponents and each was the strategist, the quarterback and the leader. It was good exercise and we got pretty good at it after awhile. I usually played on the Davis team and enjoyed hearing his Bostonian accent analyze the situation, describe the play and then execute the commands.

Navigation training was composed of two segments–the ground school training and the actual navigation training in the air. Most of our training flights were in a sturdy little plane, the AT-7. It was a twin-engine plane with a twin-finned tail section, looking a lot like a miniature B-25. There was a twin cockpit, the left chair for the pilot and the right for one of the navigation instructors. In the fuselage section were three desks in tandem. Each desk had a compass, an air speed indicator and a drift meter. Most of the training flights concentrated on dead reckoning navigation. By monitoring the airspeed, the plane's drift and understanding compass adjustments for magnetic variation and compass declination, it was possible to calculate the true heading and the true ground speed. These permitted the plotting of the plane's position on a Mercator projection map. If you did everything just right, the plotted position would be within sighting distance of the actual location. It was great fun.

After the tough courses in meteorology, the ground school classes were easy. I especially enjoyed the training in celestial navigation. We learned to identify about two dozen navigation stars and how to use the little A-20 sextant to plot a line of position and a navigational "fix." In the air it was very difficult, though, because the small planes were too unsteady a sextant platform. But we learned.

One mystery was never fully resolved. Why did the Air Force want ten navigators who were well-trained weather officers? There were two favorite theories. One was that we would be assigned to the new large bombers, the B-29's which had not yet flown a combat mission. The other was that we would do weather reconnaissance in remote sectors of the world where good weather data were lacking or too minimal to be of full use.

As we got closer to graduation day there was an increase in the talk about the best assignments, especially the planes to which we might be assigned. By that time the plane being built in greatest numbers and which required a navigator as a crew member was the B-24 Liberator being assembled in record numbers at Willow Run, Michigan, with the legendary Henry Ford riding herd. While this was the most likely assignment it was not the preferred, The vaunted Flying Fortress was the plane in the top spot. In the bottom spot was the B-26 Maurauder. This was a medium bomber, twin engined with a single tail. It was a "hot" plane, often referred to as the "Baltimore Whore," because it had no "visible means of support." The B-25 was a favorite along with the B-17. At Hondo was an instructor who had flown on a 25 in the famous 1942 mission from the decks of the aircraft carrier, Hornet. This was the raid on Tokyo that was led by Jimmy Doolittle, now a General in command of the 8th Air Force flying out of England. The

Hondo instructor on this famous flight talked at the Officer Mess about his experiences in China, where his pilot landed after bombing Tokyo. He made China seem to be an alluring and mysterious place. What an adventure he had! All during our four months of training we kept learning more and more about the B-29, the new very large bomber that was the big brother of the B-17. The 29 was designed and built by Boeing as was the 17. It looked a lot like it in side profile and had a similar name, being known as the Superfort.

Although Kush was my roommate and a good friend, it was another meteorologist in training who became my bosom buddy. He was Jack Covington. I never did figure out just what threw us together. Unlike I, he was an excellent athlete, an especially gifted track star. One of our requirements was a monthly physical performance evaluation. I could do the chin-ups and the sit ups as well as Jack. But in the 300-yard run Jack was always first and I was always last. Jack was a Texan, but from Texarkana, so was partly non-Texan. He laughed at the Texan attitude that they were winning the war single-handedly. We used to save what we called Texan headlines from the San Antonio Post. My favorite was **FLIER WHO SHOT DOWN FOUR PLANES MAY HAVE BEEN TEXAN.**

We confirmed our partnership the night we took up with the Alling sisters. We met them at one of the weekly USO dances. Jack was attracted to Evelyn and I to Margie. Those first double dates were certainly the highlight of our San Antonio social life. Mrs. Alling was pure patrician and as gracious and charming as her daughters. For about a month we were invited to stay Saturday nights at the lovely Alling home. I gradually fell in love with Margie. Jack kept a better perspective on the relationships. Margie and I would go to church on Sundays. It was an Anglican church and I began to feel that this Church was the optimum blend of my Presbyterian teachings at Sunday School and the exposure to Roman Catholic formalities that surrounded me in my four years at the University of Scranton. But all good things end too soon. Margie wanted to date other young men and she was getting ready to go back to Denton School for Women. But, even after the relationships ended Jack and I talked often about the rewards of having known the lovely Alling family for those few months.

As we approached graduation day it became obvious that Jack and I would rank #1 & #2 in the class. Jack was the best in the flight navigation evaluations and I was second. I ranked first in the ground school courses and Jack was second. We set our sights on the promised plum of assignments upon graduation. The first B-29 combat unit, the 58th Wing, under Col. Haman was in training to leave the States for some mysterious Shangri La airbase—obviously within range of some of the Japanese targets. The 58th was the first wing to be assigned to a brand new Bomber Command, the XXth, under General Wolfe The B-29's ability to fly long distances was not needed in Europe so we knew that B-29's would be deployed somewhere in the Pacific theater. We knew a lot about the B-29 program because several of the Hondo pilots had RON (remained overnight) at Smoky Hill Field, near Salina, Kansas, where the B-29 crews were training. Also, the brand new plant dedicated to the sole manufacture of B-29's was located nearby, in Wichita. Our AT-7's went there often on day-night missions.

At that time one of the qualifications for assignment to a B-29 was a dual flight rating. A pilot had to be also qualified as a flight engineer, or as a bombardier or as a navigator. We were told that two graduates of each of the classroom groups in 44-4 would be sent to bombardier school and thence to a B-29 crew assignment. Both Jack and I kept telling Captain Long that we both wanted and deserved the two selections from 44-4-4. We took it for granted that we would get these orders.

Most of the missions in our little AT-7's were short—out for two hours and back in for two hours. A few were longer and were day-night missions. We would fly out from Hondo. I still remember the coordinates, 29° 20' N and 99° 10' E. On a full gas tank we could go to places like Wichita, Enid, Memphis, Colorado Springs on these day-night missions during which we could practice our celestial navigation. The one really long mission was called the graduation mission. We flew, five students per plane, on a bigger aircraft. For us it was a trip to Van Nuys, Calif. On arrival our crew chief, very obligingly, located some "very serious" motor malfunctions that would take two days to get parts and repair. What a grand graduation present that was. We hotfooted it to Hollywood, danced in the Palladium that first night, went to CBS and NBC broadcasts the next day and then went over to Warner Brothers' Studio. We were on the set when they were shooting the movie, "To Have and Have Not." We watched the fabled Humphrey Bogart in a love scene with a gorgeous teenager named Betty Bacall. And he wasn't acting! I also met Hoagy Carmichael, whose haunting Stardust was the best known song of my teenage dancing days. Hoagy looked just like his name sounded.

At the Van Nuys Operations Office on the return trip, I watched with envy a half dozen hotshot fighter pilots who trained there and were just about ready for combat assignments. The amazing plane they flew was a new one for me, the incomparable P-51. Then it was back to Hondo. Both Sturchio and Kuhlman were given "washout" notices and off they went. We had a brief graduation ceremony on March 4. Eight of the original dozen cadets graduated. Most of them got B-24 assignments. Ten of the original fifteen lieutenants graduated. Nine of the ten were meteorology officers. The other officer, first lieutenant Michaels, drew an assignment on a B-17 crew as did my roommate, Kush. Only four of the weathermen got assignments in line with the intent of the original program that brought us to Hondo. These four were Davis and Conyers, both from Massachusetts, still retaining that rich Bostonian accent when they said farewell. The other two were Rhodes and Taylor. The four were to report to Gander for transport to the Eighth Air Force in a special role. Later we were to hear that they were assigned to duty as meteorologist-navigators aboard British DeHaviland Mosquito Bombers. But their special planes were not bombers. They were "stripped down" Mosquitoes, a relatively light weight plane, anyway, since it was made from molded plywood. These unarmed planes were flying in to Germany to collect up-to-date weather information over proposed German targets. They had only one defense—speed.

That left four graduates without definitive combat-oriented assignments. We were to become four go-fors, but with an

illustrious title—Official Liaison Meteorology Navigator Instructor Personnel Officers. My aunt Blanche wrote me a three-
page letter explaining the sexual connotation of the word Liaison. I was betrayed as was my now even better bosom buddy,
Jack. We, the most deserving, got naught. But, we became roommates and commiserated endlessly.

The other two liaison officers were delighted with the assignment. One was Lt. Newendorp. He was a great guy. One look,
and you could tell he was a descendant of the Hollanders. He
was tall and handsome with the pug nose of the Dutchers. He
had a most beautiful wife, who was great with child. Jack and I
loved the Newendorps. The fourth was Dick Miller. He had a car.
In addition he had just been married—and to a very pretty little
woman, too. Miller was okay He had a sense of humor and always helped round out our gang of four "metrogators." He, naturally, was a little bit close to his wife. But, out at the post we
would ride in his car to the little Hondo swimming hole on
those hot, hot, hot days. Richard J. would smoke his good cigars
and drink his beer and always was ready to laugh at laughing
occasions. He, Newendorp, Jack and I were a close foursome.

Jack and I affectionately labeled Kenneth E. Newendorp,
"Newdrip." I said he was a tall good-looking Dutchman, with a
most pleasant disposition. How he could rattle on a soft steady
stream and keep a conversation going always. We all liked the
guy. His damned pretty wife, Jan, was in this increasing state of
pregnancy all during our stay at Hondo, from early gestation
to pre-delivery. Her D-Day was a favorite topic of concern to
all of us.

Jack and I decided not to give up. We would try. In the meantime we went into San Antonio and sought the equivalent of the
Alling sisters. We never were that lucky again. We cleared one
entire wall of our room in the tar-papered hut where we were
quartered, and many were the pin-up pictures we displayed
there. There was the Betty Grable with her look to the photographer behind her. There was the famous shot of Rita in her neg-
ligee turning her head as she sat partly upright in her bed. We
had them all and many were the men in the BOQ who came to
admire. We determined to become the very best of the naviga-

tors ever to leave Hondo. We sought all the proficiency flights that the rules would allow. We flew the legal fifty hours a month for practice, practice, practice. Jack was better than I, but I was getting to be pretty damned good, too. We flew whenever we could... 5000 miles a month in those slow AT-7's was not out of reach. We knew we were more than ready.

We were each in different briefing schedules for teaching the cadets. In my schedule was a Lt. Jack Graham, who was in Grand Rapids with me. I was nauseated that a meteorologist could do the same job that I, a graduate of navigation school, was required to do. Graham's and my boss was Captain Klugston. We called him "Klugbutt," a not endearing term. Klugston slowly became my enemy as he resisted my efforts to get assigned to combat. Covington and I still hoped for that elusive B-29 assignment.

But the B-29 program was not going very well. The week after we graduated from the navigation program we heard a little about what was called "The Battle of Kansas." General Hap Arnold, the chief of all the Air Forces, was pissed at the many delays in getting the 58th Wing combat ready. He went to Salina himself, kicked ass and made some changes. By March 26th a dozen of these fabulous new planes were finally ready. They left Kansas on the long trip to who knew where.

I found out. We metrogators used the Hondo Weather Station as our base of operations. One morning a pilot came in for a clearance. He was a neighbor of mine back in Dunmore, Pa. He was "Frosty" Peters who had played center on the football team when we were in high school. He was now a pilot assigned to the ATC (Air Traffic Command). He had just delivered some new navitrainer equipment to Hondo. We went to lunch and he told an interesting tale. As part of his ATC duties he had made several flights "over the hump," the pilots' reference to flying over the high mountains of the Himalayas. One of his destinations on these flights had been Cheng Du, China, where he said the Chinese were building the longest runway airport anywhere in the world. Frosty's mission was to deliver aviation gasoline to this not-yet-completed air base in China. Bingo! It had to be the place where the B-29's were heading. What a flight that had to be, too.

From Smoky Hill Field to Gander, and then to Marrakesh in Africa, one of Churchill's favorite vacation spots. From thence to Cairo and on to Karachi in what is now Pakistan and then to Calcutta before flying the "hump" into Cheng Du. As soon as I could I asked Jack "How would you like to go to Cheng Du?" We went over to the map room and located this strange sounding city. It was deep in the heart of China—just like the Shangri La of the movie "Lost Horizon," one of Ronald Colman's great films of the mid-thirties. It would be a half century later before I would visit Cheng Du. The United Nations sent me there twice—to lecture to the Chinese scientists about the chemistry of silicones. There is a research institute located there today—and none of the Chinese I met had any recollection of the wartime airfields they had constructed so long ago.

In May, just two months from graduation day, we heard some chilling news. The first to die of the twenty graduates of Hondo Forty-four Four Four was Bill Davis. How could that tall strong natural leader be gone? But it was true. His Mosquito was badly damaged on its recon flight mission. To avoid pursuit and further damage the pilot had taken the plane down "on the deck." It blasted out of France and over the channel. When it caught fire the plane was so low that Davis and the two pilots hit the cold water just as their chutes were opening. Miller, Newendorp, Jack and I reviewed our memories that evening. We wrote to Taylor, who had sent us the news. Keep your feet dry! Yes, Davis was the first to die, but there would be more.

By mid-May it started to get hot every day, even in the mornings. All of us weathermen would gather in the weather office each morning after breakfast. We always had a nickel pool; Put your nickel in and predict the hour of the day when the temperature would first hit 100°. Bless Col. Davy, the Hondo C.O. He authorized short sleeves and no ties as regulation for the summer.

The biggest day of the war since Pearl Harbor was that of June 6. My future brother-in-law, Bill Nowell, and his brother were wading ashore on Omaha Beach that morning. At Hondo Jack and I were excited about the big event in Europe, but were in the doldrums.... thinking "now the war will be over soon and we will have fought only the battle of Hondo." We had meetings with our four instructors in Forty-four Four. They were lieutenants Johnson, Thomas and Williams and, of course, Captain Long. Again, they said they would put in a good word. The following week some exciting war news broke. For the first time since the daring Doolittle raid on Tokyo over two years earlier there was a bomber attack on Japan. The target was the Yawota steel plant just north of Nagasaki. Jack and I went to the map room. We measured it: from Cheng Du to Nagasaki and return was 3200 miles. Now that is some kind of navigation. Several months later I would fly group lead on the longest mission of the five year old European war. Yet it was less than half the distance of this historic bombing raid on Japan. We said over and over about navigating a 3200 mile mission, "That's for us; that's for us!!"

The reality of the situation, though, would have made us think twice. The mission of the new bomber command, the XXth, flying out of China was not that successful. On this first historic raid, for example, only half of the 80 planes that started from Cheng Du got to the Yawata target. Flying in all the gasoline "over the Hump" was more than a Herculean task. And there was no fighter escort.

That same week news of another sort started to emerge from the Pacific. In two years the Marines had invaded and captured many, many Pacific islands once held by the Japanese. In June of '44 they were at it again—this time it was Tinian. Again Jack and I went to the map room. The import of this raging battle for an island we had never heard mentioned was clear to us navigators. Tinian was only 1200 miles from <u>Tokyo</u>. Another island, Saipan lay to the south very near Tinian. And somewhat further south was an island we had heard lots about in the early days of the war. It was Guam. These were the three largest island in the Marianas. We both said to each other. Good bye China, hello Guam or Tinian. The battle for these three islands lasted more than a month. But, eventually they were secure. A little later I heard from my best high school friend, Scotty MacGregor. He was now a captain and was in charge of a bomb disposal squadron. He was busy cleaning up Tinian.

Meanwhile, back to China. General Arnold, was pissed once again. The B-29 program was faltering. He reached into his bag and extracted the youngest two star general in the Air Force. He transferred him to be in charge of the XXth Bomber Command. From the fabled Eighth came Gen. Curt Le May to shape up the B-29 program in China. He did, too. Practically his very first action was to fly a mission himself. This occurred on September 5, 1944. Later, his planes started hitting Jap targets as far north as Manchuria and as far south as Singapore. He was one tough, cigar-chomping airman.

By the fourth of July in '44, Tinian was secure. By the end of July all of the three islands were in U.S. hands. We knew that the SeaBees would be preparing those long, long runways before Scotty cleared the last mine or bomb that the Japs had planted. Maybe now Jack and I would get those B-29 assignments. We both wrote separate letters, not through channels, to Col. Davy, the C.O. And I started goofing-off, which got one desired result, a chewing out by old Klugbutt almost every day. July 31: my mother's birthday. I sent her a nice gift and Jack and I went together to buy a neat gift for Newendorp's baby—-due almost any minute now. In the evening paper was some social news. Margie Alling got married. That ends that. But fond memories!

August 4: I got them. My orders came in to report to Lincoln AAB for assignment to a B-17 crew. All of us knew a lot about the B-17. It was the first bomber to be mentioned in the war news following Pearl Harbor Day. For two years it had been carrying the war to the Germans with ever more success. I said good bye to Jack and Miller and Newendorp and took my last ride on an AT-7 to Indianapolis. From there I hitchhiked to Scranton and then it was off to Lincoln and the replacement pool. I was processed, lectured to, indoctrinated, and given orders sending me to phase training in Sioux City, Iowa.

A month later I heard from Jack. He was leaving Hondo and was getting that B-29 assignment that we had talked about so many, many times. Our correspondence tapered off. The next time I heard he had completed a whirlwind course in the bombardier school at Albuquerque. Then I was off to Italy. When

Jack wrote next it was early 1945. He was stationed in Cuba at the Guantanomo Air Base. From there he was learning to navigate the big 29 Superfort over vast expanses of water. It was much more challenging navigation than that required in a B-17 over Europe. Let's go back to China. By October '44 there were the first of what could be called very successful raids. One was on the large aircraft complex on Formosa. Another was an aircraft complex on Kyushu, the southernmost of the Japanese Islands. In December, Le May learned a valuable lesson. He was requested by superiors to carry incendiary bombs to destroy a target, a supply depot of the Japs in Northeast China at Hankow. Despite misgivings about the wisdom of using fire as a weapon instead of raw power, he complied and the mission was a success, burning over half of the targeted area. Le May never forgot the lessons of Hankow.

While Le May was shaping up the XXth the even newer XXIst Bomber Command was formed and sent to operate out of the Marianas. It was on Saipan that the Seabees completed the first of the long runways, over 1 1/2 miles long, necessary for the B-29 takeoff. New bombers were arriving weekly. By October 1944 there were enough bombers on Saipan to start flying a few "practice" missions short range to targets at Truk. The XXIst was commanded by General Hansell, a veteran B-17 wing commander flying combat out of England. More recently he had been Arnold's chief of staff for the XXth. He asked for and got Brig. General O'Donnell to head the 73rd Wing, the first of what would be dozens of combat wings on the Marianas. On my birthday, November 2, 1944, while I was on the high seas heading for Italy, the first lone B-29 ever to go over Tokyo came back with hundreds of photos and other information needed for the first B-29 raid against this militarily- and psychologically-important target. O'Donnell urged that the first raid be delayed until at least 100 bombers were ready. In the meantime practice raids against Truk continued. To complicate the buildup to 100 planes was a Japanese air raid against the Isely Field on Saipan. The Japanese planes had to have come from what would be a well-known island a few months hence.

It was Iwo Jima. You can bet that O'Donnell took his planes on other practice raids, these to Iwo.

In late November 110 B-29's were ready. Loaded with 5000 pounds of bombs and 50,000 pounds of gasoline, they needed every inch of the long runway of Isely Field in order to lumber off on the long road to Tokyo. Obviously, this was an historic mission. It was the first time that Tokyo had been bombed since the famed 30 seconds that Jimmy Doolittle's B-25's were over Tokyo almost three years earlier. But it was an historic flight in what was probably an even more important way. Meteorological history was made that day. These 100 B-29's rounded Mount Fuji and headed for the target, with some coming in from the west at altitudes up to 33,000 feet. They discovered what we now call the "jet stream." These winds, these supernatural Banshees, almost howled as they swept the planes along at breakneck speeds with tailwinds over 150 knots. At these fabulous and unexpected ground speeds most bombardiers missed sighting the target accurately. There was a minimum of damage to the target.

During December only a half dozen strikes against Japan were made. The B-29 program appeared to be in mortal danger, for losses were high and results were not commensurate. The first three weeks of January produced the same results. Once again Arnold moved Le May into the breech. He became the new commander of the XXIst.

At the end of January another runway was completed, this one on Tinian. The 313th Bombardment Wing was activated to fly from this island. A wing, at strength, could mount a strike force of 100 to 125 planes. In early February Le May experimented with some changes that moved him closer to what would become his new strategy. He sent over 100 planes to Kobe. They were to go in at 25,000 feet, below the howling fury of the wild winds aloft. And, the planes carried incendiary, rather than high explosive bombs. He remembered Hankow! This raid on Kobe was the most successful of any to date. In late February another wing, the 314th, was ready to fly from another completed runway, this one on Guam. And my Hondo roommate, Jack Covington, arrived with his B-29 crew and was assigned to the 313th flying out of a new second air-field on Tinian. Another important event occurred in February. The marines hit the "Sands of Iwo Jima"!

Le May did two more things of import. He doubled the train-ing time for each of the radar navigators. He had heard of the fabulous success of the Fifth Wing, my wing of B-17's in Italy, when we knocked out the big B, Brux, on Christmas day '44—using Radar to bomb through a solid overcast which hid Brux from visual view. The second thing Le May did was send a dozen planes on a practice mission, bombing at fifty feet altitude. Later, a crew member exaggerated slightly, in reporting that one of the bombs had bounced up from the ground fifty feet and was flying formation off his wingtip. Soon Le May was convinced that his crews could bomb effectively from low altitude, and us-ing radar, could bomb with a solid cloud cover, or at night.

Jack Covington's first combat mission was on March 9. At the briefing he heard the plan, which was as close to terrifying as a plan could be. The planes were going to go in over Tokyo at night and below 10,000 feet. In addition they were carrying a new kind of fire bomb, a bomb containing napalm. A DuPont chemist had discovered that he could make a jellied sticky in-cendiary material by adding sodium palmitate to gasoline. The chemical symbol for sodium is Na, ergo, napalm. At lower alti-tudes the B-29 did not need the reserve fuel carried in the bomb bay tanks so a much larger bomb load, double the poundage of previous missions, was possible. The planes were to go in by threes, so even the comfort of a dozen or more nearby planes would be missing. Le May borrowed the RAF practice of first sending in pathfinder planes, to form a fiery cross over the cen-ter of Tokyo. Two weeks earlier the RAF had destroyed the city of Dresden in a fiery maelstrom using this same technique. Sub-sequent planes used the pathfinder fires as a guide to their own bombing pattern. Using the intervalometers the bombardier distributed a napalm bomb every fifty feet. They carried 180 bombs on each plane. Three wings flew that mission—over 300 B-29's. They bombed Tokyo for a total of three hours and set fif-teen square miles ablaze. Le May had found a strategy that would end the war.

The morality of this strategy is still debated. More civilians in Tokyo were killed in this first fire raid than would die at Hiroshima just five months later. Ending the war through these terrorist bombings saved 500,000 American lives and probably 2 million Japanese who would have died if an invasion of Japan were required to end the fanatical Japanese resistance. The real question is probably, "Is any war justified?" or "Is every murderous act in a justified war justified?" Generals, like self-styled humanitarians, come to different conclusions. My old boss, General Eaker, commander of the Mediterranean Allied Air Forces, was dead set against terrorist civilian bombing. We, in the 15th Air Force, had the word. General Le May was not against such a weapon. He ended the war early.

Covington would fly four more of these fire raid missions in the next two weeks. He really earned his air medal. Later in March he would fly a few easier missions—against kamikaze air bases in Kyushu. The fleet was under kamikaze attack as they softened Japanese defenses of Okinawa, before the Marines would storm ashore on April 1. On March 27 Jack flew the first of some missions he liked best. The 313th was assigned the task of mining dozens of harbors and straits from Tokyo and Yokohama on Honshu to Sasebo on Kyushu. This program was amazingly successful. No more raw material would flow into Japan until after the war.

More than once the Marines "bailed out" the Army. The panache of the Marines required they would help the helpless Army with a little more than disdain. It was expressed best much earlier in the Pacific war when the Marines used to sing, what for them was a gentle song:

We asked for the Army on Guadalcanal,
But General MacArthur said "no."
He gave as his reason
" It's the rainy season,
Besides there is no USO."

For the beleaguered Army Air Force B-29 combat crews, who fought in the mold, in fact in the epitome of that courageous mold, of the Marines' valor, the Marines never did more for the Army than secure the "Sands of Iwo Jima." The Marines paid a bitter price. Over 7,000 Marines gave "that last full measure of devotion" to secure the island. But, more than 20,000 B-29 crewmen landed in distraught airplanes on Iwo in the last several months of the war. There they could get repairs at "Rocky's Wayside Station" and get back to their Marianas Islands to fly once more, and once more do damage to the Japanese—damage that would save the lives of many, many Marines. What goes around comes around. Jack Covington was one of these beleaguered B-29 crewmen. His plane barely made it to Iwo, after terrific damage while dropping mines over Japan's lifeline, the Shimonoseki Straits. Jack was almost dumfounded to see the operation for repairing B-29's that was active on Iwo when his plane was there. There were almost 100 B-29's being repaired on Iwo at that time. It looked like another bombardment wing. Jack and his crew flew their renewed plane back to Tinian two days later.

By mid May, with Okinawa secure, the 29's could end the campaign against the kamikaze airfields. Le May renewed the successful fire attacks. The last fire attack on Tokyo was also Jack's last and fatal flight. On May 24, in this last massive raid on the heart of Japan, over 500 B-29's participated. Because the emperor's residence was in the target area the defense was fanatical. The XXIst suffered its worst losses. Over a hundred planes were damaged and 25 were lost—including Covington's plane and crew. But Tokyo was now destroyed. It was never a target again. Jack, thus, was the last member of Hondo Forty-four Four Four to die in combat. For three months he was in the center of the whirlwind that Japan reaped. He more than helped end the war early. In two more months a lone B-29 would complete the destruction of Japan's psychological will to continue the war Japan started on a fiery morning of the December day that "lives in infamy." The B-29's ended that war.

EPILOGUE

Ninety-one seniors graduated from the University of Scranton in June 1942. We were the "between the wars class," most born just after WWI and the first to graduate after the USA entered WWII.

Almost all of the graduates joined a branch of military service. Our generation fought and ended the war. It was an extension of our younger careers which were forged in the delights of the twenties and honed in the realities of the "Great Depression." We were ready for the war.

Ours was the first generation, too, wherein many poor young men could be and were well educated. We led the nation to victory in war, to preeminence in science, medicine, the arts, and business prowess. In our later years we sense the denouement. We must let go.

BIBLIOGRAPHY

Jablonski, Edward. *Flying Fortress.* Doubleday and Company, Inc., 1965.

Osborne, Charles, et al. *World WarII.* Time-Life Books, Inc., 1976.

Irving, David. *The Destruction of Dresden.* New York: Holt, Rinehart and Winston, 1963.

...about the author.

The author enlisted in the flight program of the U.S. Army Air Corps the day after he graduated from the University of Scranton in 1942. He was one of twenty premed students in the class of '42. He flew eighteen missions with the Fifteenth Air Force in 1944 and 1945 and was awarded the Air Medal with oak leaf cluster and the Prisoner of War medal.

He obtained his Ph.D. in Chemistry from Pennsylvania State University in 1948 and joined Dow Corning Corporation as a Research Chemist. He became Research Director and Vice President in 1973 and retired in 1983. He may be the only 72-year-old author with four children still in college. Three other children have completed college and all seven think his first book "is terrific."

✪

Wild Blue Yonder may be ordered
from Publishers Distribution Service
by calling 1-800-345-0096 (toll free)
or 1-616-929-0733 (in Michigan & outside U.S.)
or by FAX 1-616-929-3808

or by writing to:
Publishers Distribution Service
121 East Front Street, Suite 203
Traverse City, MI 49684

———————

Quantity discounts are available.

Visa and Mastercard accepted.